Salem Secret Underground
The History of the Tunnels in the City

by
Christopher Jon Luke Dowgin

Salem, Massachusetts

Salem, Massachusetts

Salem House Press
Salem, Ma
Whiting, NJ
First Published 2012

Salem House Press
P.O Box 249
Salem, Ma 01970

1481 Newark Ave.
Whiting, N.J. 08759

Salem House Press™ and logo is a registered trademark

ISBN-10 0983666555 ISBN-13 9780983666554
First Edition: 2nd Printing

Visit our tour "A Walk Under Salem and Salem Secret Underground" on Google Maps to follow the path of the tunnel while you are walking in Salem or the privacy of your own home. Also book a tour on the Salem Tunnel Tour to learn about them first hand. www.salemtunneltour.com

Introduction

Smuggling is an ancient and well respected art. Committed by pirates and thieves and sometimes politicians. Well, in Salem the politicians were the best pirates; I beg your pardon, I mean privateers and thieves. By no means was Salem the only sea front town who was making a fortune underground, most towns that sat on the waterfront had tunnels leading away from their wharfs. From Maine to N.J. smuggling was a common occurrence stretching way back into the 1600's. Then again Salem was on top of the game where smuggling through tunnels was above board making it the city to have the first and the most millionaires in the country during the 18th century.

Smuggling in the Colonies can at least be dated back to 1680 when New Jersey residents fought the attempts of Gov. Andros to instill duties upon commerce that sailed the Delaware. The argument even back then was taxation without representation. In 1699 British vice-admiral Robert Quarry wrote "*apprehended 4 Pyrates at Cape May. I might have with ease secured the rest of them and the ship too had not the local officials entertained the Pyrates, conveyed them from place to place, furnished them with provisions and liquors, given them intelligence and sheltered them from justice. All the persons that I have employed in searching for and apprehending these Pyrates are abused and affronted and called enemies to the country for disturbing and hindering honest men.*" In New York if they paid their protection money to Gov. Fletcher of £100 per man smugglers were given the keys to the city. Captains and merchants had to pay even higher fees and Fletcher welcomed bribery. The pirate Captain Tew rode often in his carriage at high noon and was his favorite dinner guest. So it can be assumed that in Salem this persisted in such early times as can be seen by the tunnels leading to and from the Daniel's House that was built in 1667. Indeed the "smuggling Interest" became a factor of great political strength in the trading towns in the north colonies.

In England respectable gentlemen of position ad rank thought it only custom to smuggle. King Edward III tried imposing an exportation tax on wool which only exasperated the smuggling from English ports to Danish ones. Even after King Charles II tried ending smuggling, they eventually came to the conclusion that policing it was a dead issue.

In 1733 England passed the Molasses Act. Molasses was a favorite commodity for smuggler's to pass under the crown's nose. See molasses and sugar was 25% to 40% cheaper in French Guadeloupe, Martinique, and Spanish Santo Domingo than they were in the British West Indies. The British controlled islands of Jamaica, Antigua, and Barbados were too expensive for Colonists to make honest profits on. Now these Island planters lived mostly in London and cried extensively to the crown about falling profits which resulted in a tax of six cents per gallon on non-British island molasses. After the passing of this act in the Colonies, smuggling just became more active, creative, and profitable to custom officials. James Otis in N.J. had said "a very small office in customs has raised a man a fortune sooner than a post in government." It has been said that needy wretches will find it easier and more profitable not only wink but sleep in their beds; the merchants pay being more generous than the King's. Another acquired trick was to mislabel the cargo to that which was not taxable. Sometimes captains could pay duties on 8 barrels of rum in one port and gain receipts. Then they would sail to another port and take on 72 more barrels and then add a "y" to eight on the receipt to make it eighty barrels that have been paid for. Other tricks were to fix the ship logs to show only partial entries of the cargo. So amidst the Molasses Act it was very profitable to buy from the French.

Then war broke out with the French in 1756. During the French and Indian War smuggling with the French became treason. Alas, the French was paying through the nose for Colonial goods! When you could invest 10 shillings and make 3 pounds, many thought the risk was well worth having your neck stretched for ye. Gov. Morris of Pennsylvania roamed the waterfront himself forcing in windows and doors to stop the smuggling to little effect. The smugglers resembled a hydra, once you cut one head off another popped up to replace it. In 1759 Thomas Penn reported to the crown that French Shallops had swarmed Philadelphia and were unloading illegal cargo under flags of truce that the French paid dearly for to the right officials. Not only were they unloading but bringing back money and provisions to France to fight the Brits with. Some of this money and provisions would go towards the killing of colonist in New York state who signed up for the British army to fight the French.

Now King George III came to the throne penniless after the wars with France and appointed George Greenville to change this. It was commonly noticed in Virginia and New York that the populace kept up with the latest fashion, locution, and dance that hit London. Servant girls were dressed as good as their mistresses. The colonies were a land of health, wealth, plenty and contentment in the 1760's and George was going to make what he thought would be his fortunes on the colonies. One of England's tragic faults were when one part of their empire was failing they would have another colony sure it up often leading to problems in the colony to be fixed later. At this point the East India Trading Company was faltering. Now Greenville who would only lasted 2 years in position took action to profit in the America's which would lead to war.

The old Navigational Acts of 1651 were enforced and now policed by the British Navy. This meant that any Colonial imports had to sail to British ports first to be taxed before they sailed to their final destination. Previous it was said that his majesty's government paid 8,000 pounds a year to collect 2,000 pounds in duties a year. Greenville calculated that they were missing 700,000 pounds a year to be found in the Americas. No longer could the smugglers not worry about this act without consequences in which their grandfathers scoffed at. Also at this time manufacturing was almost outlawed in the colonies relinquishing to the colonies that position of being an agriculture realm only. Forcing them to buy British manufactured goods at inflated prices without fear of competition.

The hardest hit to the smugglers were the new Sugar Act in 1764. The Brits were being nice though. They originally wanted to tax six pence per gallon of molasses but decided to only tax 3 pence. They were feeling amicable. Though the colonial merchant still had to pay 3 pence more per gallon than he had to. Now this tax went back into British Troops who were posted in the colonies to patrol smugglers.

This with new Scottish laddys who were content to live on salaries alone collecting the duties removed almost all of the smuggler's friends, hard times had come to the colonies. All imports flooded into the British islands dropping prices creating a depression in the colonies. Lot of colonial goods rotted in warehouses and on ports with no market. Rum would soon become a luxury item that the poorer folk could only use in small amounts for medicinal purposes.

Soon colonial ports were moved up smaller rivers that the crown never heard of and to islands never used before. Also in 1764 in NJ Gov. William Franklin had reported to the Lords of Trade that customs agents had entered a deal with the merchants where they paid a dollar a hogshead for sugar and molasses in lieu of duties passes by act of Parliament. William's father Benjamin would later write in 1770 "The English never hesitated to avoid payments on duties when they could, even though they made their own laws, as the Americans had not." The British efforts fell through. The new Stamp Act did not help them, but exasperated the Americans even more.

By 1766 an American Board of Commissioners of Customs was set up on paper to appoint searchers, collectors, surveyors, clerks, and informers. Plus laws were changed to gather more convictions. Those people who applied for these jobs were harassed by neighbors before they could receive their first pay, witnesses lost their memory, and juries denied convictions. When John Hancock's ship the Liberty was seized in 1768 the customs house in Boston was protested with such a large mob that Hancock was free to unload his cargo with the help of a large free labor force. Then the mob marched to the Comptroller of Customs house, Benjamin Hallowell, and smashed his windows and burned his barge on the Boston Commons in front of Hancock's house. America's largest smuggler Hancock was fined 100,000 pounds which was never collected and the legal case around him fell apart. Francis Hopkinson was appointed in 1763 Collector of Customs in Chansey, NJ and would later become one of the signers of the Declaration of Independence. Also it is said he was the original designer of the American flag and not Betsy Ross.

Since 1775 at the beginning of the War, privateers had made the long profession of pirating legal. A privateer was a ship privately owned, armed, provisioned, and bearing a marque from the State or the Continental Congress to attack an enemies commerce to be sold at auction with the profits distributed amongst owners, officers, and crew. A lowly sailor on such a voyage could even make $1,000 plus wages. One author called it "The most profitable racket in the world-as long as you do not get your throat cut." The first to take up this title was Captain Joseph White who had 3 of his ship taken by the British. In a conversation with the Cabot brothers of Beverly he had said he would have his revenge and go a privateering. The Cabots and Captain White bought a ship from Elias Hasket Derby called "Come along Patty" a sloop he renamed "Revenge"! Captain White commanded the ship with 50 men and ten guns and was the first privateer to sail from Salem. Two hundred and sixty seven ships sailed from Salem during the war. 10,000 men sailed out of Salem and Beverly on ships of these privateers. Plus, countless shallops sailed out in the morning and returned prizes by the evening. Most square rigged ships sailing from Salem were captured (66%) but the sloops were the most successful in bringing in prizes. The most notable privateers from Salem were John Fiske, Jonathan Haraden, William Gray, John Revell, John Derby, Joseph

Waters, David Ropes, Nathaniel West, Simon Forrester, Thomas Simmons, Lieut. Joseph Peabody, James Barr, Samuel Ingersoll, and Thomas Perkins. In 1778 Alderman Woodbridge told the House of Lords that 733 ships were lost to privateers resulting in a loss of $10,000,000 since the beginning of the Revolutionary War. By American records from 1776 to 1782 privateers took 1,2000 ships causing $20,000,000 in losses to the British. To the ire of the British, the skill of the colonial privateer was largely due in part by the British using them against the French in the early 1700's. The Continental Congress even had the Secret Committee of Trade that was headed by congressman Morris who made huge profits from it at a loss to Washington's army.

A side note expressing how important Molasses was, on August 20, 1829 was the first vessel that sailed from Salem that did not have liquor on board.

Now back to Elias Hasket Derby. He had 158 shares on the 267 privateers sailing from Salem during the Revolutionary War. He was a strong Loyalist until a British ship confiscated one of his ships and cargos and then he preceded to show his true colors and became a staunch supporter of the colonialist cause. His ship the Grand Turk had captured 25 ships which was the most prizes from any ships in between the years 1781 and 1782. She was also the first American ship to sail to Canton mastered by Thomas Perkins who became infamous right before the Opium War. Also John Hodges would sail the Grand Turk at one point. The gluttony of tea on the market made China unmarketable till the illicit opium trade opened up leading to the Opium War. After 1790 Derby never sent another vessel to China, but Perkins did on his own. Derby's wealth was only second to the Cabots of Beverly who bought the Revenge along with Captain Joseph White. Elias even acted as a proponent merchant agent on behalf of White and his marines regarding the capture of the brigantine Anna Maria.

Other captains sailing for Derby were Jonathan Ingersoll, Ebenezer West, and Samuel Derby. William Gray worked in the counting room for Elias Hasket Derby's father Richard.

Now Elias Hasket Derby Married Elizabeth Crowninshield and George Crowninshield married Mary Derby who was Elias' sister. Elizabeth was George's sister. Elias' eldest daughter Elizabeth married Captain Nathaniel West. By 1806 this marriage ended in an ugly divorce in which she was awarded part of a house which was removed to the current site of the North Shore Mall in Peabody. It was added to the country seat that was owned by her father Elias. Elias' other daughter Antis married Benjamin Pickman.

In 1799 The Salem East India Marine Society was formed of men that sailed beyond the Cape of Good Hope or Cape Horn as masters or supercargoes. In 1800 there members were:

James Barr Jr.
Benjamin Bullock
John Burchmore
Jonathan Carnes
Benjamin Carpenter
Henry Clarke
Benjamin Crowninshield
Clifford Crowninshield
Samuel Derby

Henry Elkins
John Felt
Richard Gardener
John Gibaut
Daniel Hathorne
Benjamin Hodges
George Hodges
Jonathan Hodges
Jonathan Ingersoll
William Ives
Jonathan Lambert
Samuel Lambert
Benjamin Lander
Jonathan Mason
Ichabod Nichols
Josiah Orne
John Osgood
John Prince Jr.
Thomas Putnam
William Richardson
William Robinson
John Ropes
Joseph Ropes
Nathaniel Silsbee
George Gilder Smith
Enoch Swett
Moses Townsend
Benjamin Webb Jr.
Edward West
ISr.ael Williams

Benjamin Hodges was their first president and sailed the Astrea and the Grand Turk for Elias Hasket Derby. In 1867 they merged a couple of museums to become the

Peabody Academy of Sciences. Today they still have their clubhouse with double passkeys on top of the Hawthorne Hotel. The property that was conveyed to them from later member Thomas Perkins. To tell you the truth, I have not realized if the Salem Marine Society and the Salem East India Marine Society are on in the same yet, but the Salem Marine Society resides on top of the Hotel.

Now in Salem after the war came a split amongst the populace. Many were Jeffersonian Democratic-Republicans and the others were Hamilton Federalists. To this day you still see this split in the remaining architecture in downtown Salem. If one was to walk up Derby Street from Congress heading toward the Willows you first see stately brick buildings mainly built in the Federalist style. Then as you head past Daniel's Street the architecture changes. A few Federalist brick buildings sneak in even though. See with better statistics, stronger ships, better charts, and insurance man finally had a sense that he was in charge or even more powerful than nature. Nature had been conquered after a long hard battle. To express this belief, Federalists created an architecture that covered the exposed beams, wooden fireplace covers with fine carvings hiding the bricks, wall paper, and had higher ceilings. Homes were no longer going to show anything in the home that was natural without feeling the heavy hand of man. Plus, they had enough revenue not to worry about the extra heating costs associated with higher ceilings. To the opposite the Jeffersonians loved nature and thought man was part of the natural order. As you roam about Daniel's, English, or say Bently you will still notice brick fireplaces, brick walls, exposed beams, and low ceilings. I find them much more homey even in the 21st century. I wonder if Duck Rogers would agree...

The Federal Movement first appeared in response to the countries inability to rise out of our poor economical times arising from paying back our war debts. The Articles of Confederation was in favor of states rights over the nation. James Madison and Alexander Hamilton wrote 85 anonymous essays called the Federalist Papers to convince New Yorkers to vote for the new Constitution favoring a centralized government. At the time it was a battle of the farmer who wanted a federated government versus the seaboard merchants who wanted a centralized government limiting states rights. Those who opposed the new Constitution and strength of the new Federal Government had complained that the Federalists forgot to include the Bill of Rights into the Constitution as they promised. These Anti-Federalist like the "Federal Farmers" and the "Federal Republican Party" were called unpatriotic. Previously the term Federal was applied to any person who supported the colonial union and the government formed under the Articles of Confederation. The anti-federalist wanted a federal government and not the centralized government that the Federalist were pushing for. Anti-Federalists worried that the Constitution would hinder individual rights and create a monarchy. Previous to Washington the various presidents of the Articles of Confederation had limited powers. They were afraid of what powers this new president would have. In opposition to these comments the Federalist pushed forth the national sentiment if you were not for them you were against them for they were the only true patriots. The strongest supporters of the Anti-Federalists were Patrick Henry, Samuel Adams, James Monroe, and Richard Henry Lee. The debate grew great with a civil war almost breaking out in Rhode Island on July 4th 1788 until the Massachusetts Compromise. The

Massachusetts Compromise forced the issue of a Bill of
Rights to be included after New York, New Hampshire,
and Virginia demanded the same. In 1787 the Constitution
was ratified and went into operation in 1789 with 12
amendments which would later be called the Bill of Rights.

After the passing of the Constitution the Federalist and
the Anti-Federalist faded away with yet the Federalist Party
rising in their wake. This one was headed by Alexander
Hamilton which became the first political party in the
country amidst George Washington's warnings of a two
party system of government. Hamilton created The New
York Post as a propaganda mouthpiece. The Federalist Party
was in open resistance of an agricultural ruled government
for a mercantile one. In response to this the Democratic-
Republican Party was formed which felt that a strong
centralized government over a federal one would be a
threat to civil liberties. The Democratic-Republican Party
feared that the national debt created by the new government
under the Constitution would bankrupt the country, and that
Federalist bondholders were paid from honest farmers and
workingmen. Part of the national debt was incurred by the
inability of the Continental Congress to pay veterans so they
issued them bonds in lieu of salaries. This was a burden
that the states had to pay back. Many veterans sold these
bonds cheap leaving a group of speculators open to making
a fortune as soon as Hamilton could have a centralized
government assume a national debt. Jefferson was against
this since his state had already paid most of its debt and
thought that those states who had the ability to pay but
choose not to would be shifting the responsibility of paying
them onto others through a national debt. It felt to him
that his state would be charged twice for another's failure.
The zenith of the Federalist Party was the election of John

Adams to president.

Also Hamilton pushed for a centralized bank called Bank of North America in 1781 and the First Bank of the United States followed it in 1791. These two banks along with Hamilton's Bank of New York were the first to be issued shares in the New York Stock Exchange. This new central bank had Robert Morris deposit large quantities of gold and silver coin and bills of exchange obtained through loans from the Netherlands and France. It was important to gain credit with the Netherlands because you needed good credit with them to fund any possible future war for most provisioners and arms supplier looked to the Netherlands to ascertain your credit. Then the bank issued paper currency backed by these amounts. This was the beginning of credit and paper circulation in the United States. The Bank of North America operated principally in three states and lost its status in Pennsylvania, 1785, because it had been seen to have "alarming foreign influence, fictitious credit, favoritism to foreigners, and unfair competition against less corrupt State Banks issuing their own bills of credit." With a change of government in Pennsylvania it was re-chartered but hindered in 1787. The National Banks are all closed today but survive in the designation from the Office of the Comptroller of Currency in the U.S. Treasury of National Association of Banks. They are protected by federal law and do not fall under state usury laws that are designed to limit predatory lending. Citibank is such an example of a N.A. or National Bank.

The fall of the Federalists came when John Adams and Charles Pickney's pro-centralized government and pro-British Federalist Party lost to the pro-French and pro-decentralized government of the Democratic-Republicans of Thomas Jefferson and Aaron Burr. One of the chief complaints of the election was opposition to imposed taxes to pay for the new army and navy sent to fight the French during the X,Y,Z affair in 1798. John Adams never recovered from his reception from the French when he was sent on diplomatic mission to France where Franklin was a dandy and he was a cold fish. When Adams felt the French gave him insult during a diplomatic mission in 1798 to bring about a truce between the British, French, and Americans after the American Revolutionary War. John Adams used the insult to force through Congress the creation of the first standing centralized army and navy along with the creation of the Alien and Sedition Acts. To settle the dispute after letters of marque were given to French and American privateers during the X, Y,Z affair to be used to harass each other the French had asked for 50,000 pounds sterling, a $12 million loan, and a $250,000 personal bribe to French foreign minister Charles Maurice de Talleyrand, and a formal apology for comments also made by Adams during the bilateral peace negotiations with the British. Adams negotiated this peace with the French later in 1799 and championed the cause for a formation of the Navy and Army.

The Alien and Sedition Acts, written by Salem's Col. Pickering who resigned afterwards, were four bills passed in 1798 that were designed to protect the United States from enemy aliens and seditious acts from weakening the government. The Democratic-Republicans denounced them as being unconstitutional and created to quite opposition of his administration which hindered on the rights of states to act in these areas. Also the acts threatened new immigrants from having a political opinion. The one of the first acts of this and the new standing army was to roust Benjamin Franklin's grandson and his newspaper the

"American Aurora" who was printing articles in opposition to the Federalists. Also he had complained "the blind, bald, crippled, toothless, querulous ADAMS" of nepotism and monarchical ambition. Benjamin Franklin Bache died while waiting for trial in jail for libel of yellow fever. This happened 2 weeks prior to the passing of the Alien and Sedition Acts came into effect. Also Hamilton had all but one of the Democratic-Republican newspapers in NY close. This last one reported that Hamilton had tried to buy the "American Aurora" to close it down. Hamilton arrested the owner Mre. Greenleaf for seditious libel who was compelled to close his "New Daily Advertiser" after his prosecution. The writing was on the wall already.

What also crippled the Federalist Party was the split between Hamilton and Adams in the election. What seems common politics now was fought the fiercest between Hamilton and Adams with smear campaigns and propaganda. The result was that Jefferson and Burr came up on top.

Then came the next problem. Now the Electoral College would vote for the President with the second largest number of votes would become vice-president. It was planned for one delegate to withhold a vote to allow Jefferson to be president and Burr vice-president. This did not go as planned and resulted in a tie that took 2 weeks for the outgoing House of Representatives which was controlled by the Federalists to choose. Alexander Hamilton detested both candidates but he could stomach Jefferson more. So he lobbied against Burr who ignored the whole affair and attended his daughters wedding in February of 1801. To ire Hamilton even more in 1804 Burr proposed himself to be the Federalist candidate for president forcing Hamilton's pride to remove himself from the Federalist. Along with all of this and allegations of improper relations between Burr and his daughter had led to the famous duel between the two in 1804. The Jefferson Presidency and the death of Hamilton brought the end of the Federalist Party, but not their sentiments which can be felt in the GOP today. Around the time of George W. Bush's inauguration in 2000 a biography of John Adams topped the NY Times Best seller List. The Alien & Sedition Act would return as Homeland Security and the government and its agencies would become even more centralized. As the supporters of Adams used double speak utilizing the popular term "Federalist" the GOP would corrupt the term "Patriot".

Now back in 1801 Elias Hasket Derby Jr. took over the Second Corp of Cadets. Then he raised $2,500 to put the Commons in better condition for a training field. Lombardy poplars were first planted to be replaced in 1818 by large elms. A wooden fence was erected around the commons afterward. Now the Commons was quite marshy, uneven, had a few hills, and several small ponds. Derby had the hills taken down and filled in the swamps and ponds. Why? Could it have been to hide all of the dirt many of his acquaintances and himself dug up during the building of yet another generation of smuggling tunnels? What spurred this on? Derby was a Federalist and was not sure which way the country was going to go with Jefferson in office.

In league with Derby was one Associate Supreme Court Justice, the Secretary of the Navy, U.S. Representatives, and 3 senators. Also in 1791 Elias Hasket Derby Jr. is one of several Salem citizens to petition for another charter to open a Mason lodge. After a serious loss in members during the Revolutionary War the original Salem Essex Lodge was closed in 1786. Now Derby along with Joseph Hiller, William Bentley, Edward Pulling, Robert Foster, James King, Benjamin Hodges, John Becket, Abel Lawrence, Benjamin W. Crowninshield, John Jenks, Jonathan Mason Jr., Benjamin Carpenter, John Page, and Joseph Vincent became its leading brethren. Joseph Hiller was the Master of the Essex Lodge with Derby as Senior Warden. Now most of these members were sea captains. Benjamin Carpenter was Master of the Salem East India Marine Society. Benjamin Hodges was the first president of the Salem East India Marine Society and his son Jonathan was its first secretary. Benjamin W. Crowninshield was Secretary of the Navy under Madison and Monroe. John Page was once Col. of the Salem Regiment and Weigher and Gauger in the Custom House. Abel Lawrence once commanded the Salem Cadets and was a distiller. Their lodge was in another distillers home, across the street from Lawrence's distillery, in the Joshua Ward house. Ward's mother was Elias' aunt. Now if there is one thing the Masons were known for was how to make a good smuggling tunnel. Now with all of these fine persons on board with ready capital they were going to make a very fine extension of tunnels through town.

Now Jefferson was busy in Washington. Jefferson is weakening the Federalist stance in government. Hamilton is not dead yet and the Federalist are still strong in the judiciary. Jefferson did not believe we needed to build debt to build foreign credit. He also found that to carry the national debt any longer would only support a "cesspool of corruption and rottenness, closing with the Revolution". Jefferson also eliminated the Whiskey tax that led to the Whiskey Rebellion in which Hamilton led troops through the Appalachians. Jefferson believed that the government could rely exclusively on customs revenue and needed no

direct taxation. Something the merchants of Salem was
not favorable for, even though the rest of the country was
against higher taxes and a strong central government.
Relying on duties on customs became harder when trade
was disturbed by the Napoleonic Wars. From 1801 to 1810
Salem paid customs duties of $7,272,633.31. Salem was safe
from the effects of the Napoleonic War at the time since they
relied on trade from the orient. Jefferson also reduced the
size of the military in which he felt was a unnecessary drain
on the public finances. Then he downsized the navy. In the
wake of that he did feel that the country needed professional
officers to lead an army of citizen soldiers when the need
arises as it did during the Revolution so he created the Army
Corp of Engineers and the Military Academy at West Point
in 1802.

When the opportunity arose Jefferson still kept most of
the Federalists in positions of the government thinking that
moderates would join the Democratic-Republican party
which they did. Only New England and Delaware kept
strong Federalist ties. John Adams retired and Hamilton
was killed leaving the Federalist with no leader to follow so
they fell apart. Only thing left was the Midnight Judges that
Adams stacked into the newly created seats in the Circuit
Courts before he left office.

In 1808 Jefferson banned the international trade in
slaves. It still continued though but fell from 14,000 slaves
per year to 1,000 a year being sold. Captain Joseph White
was a slave trader who was going to suffer losses from this
ban. Captain White had once said " I have no reluctance
in selling any part of the human race." Wednesday May
29 in 1789 Captain William Fairfield who was in White's
employment was murdered by revolting slaves while in

Africa on the brigantine Eliza. Elias Hasket Derby Sr.. was on the different, when his ship the Grand Turk first sailed to the Gold Coast he refused it to accept slaves onboard for sale. Slavery was unfavorable in Salem, but it did occur.

Prostitution was popular on Derby Street going way back. My friend in her 60's even mentioned her father warned her stay away from the area where the Pig's Eye and Witches Brew are while she was in her teens. These taverns had many tunnels they would shanghai sailors into. Derby Street sat on the waterfront and had quite an advantage to shanghai these young men. Drop him a mickey and off he goes to sea. More respectful gentlemen of town could venture through the tunnels to the brothels without being seen. So the north might not agree with slavery of Africans, but white women and young white men were fair game once they enter the tavern...

Then came the Barbary War where Jefferson's Mosquito Fleet did not fare as well as Adam's navy would in which he bribed the Barbary Pirates $60,000 to declare a victory for himself. Along with the French and English the Barbary Pirates had confiscated many ships and pressed many of our sailors into their own navies for almost a hundred years. There were countless articles from the times mentioning ships confiscated and prisoners taken from Salem in local papers. Following that in Jefferson's second term the British impressed 6,000 sailors from American ships they confiscated to man their own navy against the French during the Napoleonic War. Off the coast of Virginia the British warship Leopard tried to search The Chesapeake which ended with shots being fired and leaving 3 dead and 18 wounded American sailors. In response Jefferson passed the Embargo Act in 1807. The British already banned their exports from Europe in 1806 and the French barred anyone from selling to Europe as well in 1807. The neutrality of American ships selling to both countries left them open to seizure by both parties. The Embargo Act in 1807 passed by Jefferson forbade American ships and goods leaving American ports except for those vessels in coastal trade, in the Navy, or approved by Jefferson. This was an act to hurt Britain and France economically after they had harassed our shipping concerns overseas. Those who traded along the eastern seaboard had to a bond as a guarantee that the cargo would be delivered to an American port. This only increased the amount of smuggling going on which Jefferson openly opposed by having the navy patrol the coast and cutting off the shipping route to Canada. Also no ship could be loaded without the approval of the customs officer and the Navy. Also to limit loopholes extra measures where taken resulting in 2 supplementary acts of 1808 which allowed customs officials to call out the militia to help enforce the embargo. In Salem the militias were commanded by the shipping merchants in town like Elias Hasket Derby Jr. . The most successful merchants in Salem then where Elias Hasket Derby Jr., William Gray and Joseph Peabody. William Gray had sided with Jefferson and left behind his Federalist friends and supported the Embargo Act and moved to Boston in 1809. This brought the end to Salem's heyday that followed the Revolutionary War. In 1807 Salem had 152 ships and then after the Embargo Act and the future War of 1812 there were only 57 left in 1815. In 1807 when the Embargo Act was passed the total U.S. exports reached $108 million. Within the year they fell to $22 million. The Embargo Act lost Jefferson his 3rd presidency in 1808 and dissolved as he left office.

In 1808 James Madison the father of the Constitution

became the 4th president. He had written the Federalist
Papers with Hamilton but he broke free from him in 1791 to
help Jefferson form the Democratic-Republican Party. That
same year he wrote the first ten of the twelve Bills of Rights.
Madison agreed with Jefferson that the Constitution should
give the Federal Government less powers than Hamilton felt
it should have. Hamilton thought the Constitution should
have implied powers designed to let the government operate
as it felt it should. Later Madison would craft the Kentucky
and Virginia Resolutions in 1798 to protest the Alien and
Sedition Acts created by the Federalist under John Adams.
The First Bank of the United States charter had expired in
his term in 1811. Then due to the long standing practice of
impressing American sailors into the Royal Navy, Madison
led us into the War of 1812. England found it easy to have
volunteers sail the Royal Navy but during war most of these
experienced sailors joined merchant or privateer ships. So
the English turned to impressing American sailors who
had been born in England calling them deserters. In 1805
it was estimated that there was 9,000 sailors on U.S. ships
born in Britain. Along with impressments they prevented
our ships from doing commerce with France which was
legal again after the Embargo Act in 1808 was lifted. The
English people were fearing the growing economic power
of American mercantile and commercial competition.
Plus the British was arming Indian tribes in the Northwest
territory. The American people elected a "War Hawk"
Congress led by Henry Clay and John C. Calhoun. These
war hawks called for war but then denied Madison's call for
an expanded navy. Daniel Webster was elected to the House
of Representatives in 1812 by the Federalists shipping
interest against the war. England's navy was going to be
busy blockading European ports from the French as they
continued on with the Napoleonic War and going to war

with America.

On our continent we went to war against a combined
army of 6,034 British Force along with Canadians and First
Nation tribes which were able to capture Detroit and burn
the capital down on August 24th 1814. After Napoleon
was defeated in 1814 the British had more troops free to
deal with the Americans. In 1814 Benjamin Crowninshield
was appointed Secretary of the Navy. He would keep this
position until 1818 under James Monroe. At sea Salem also
sent many privateers to fight in the battle gaining many
prizes.

In 1813 the USS Essex captained by David Porter sailing
from Salem was sent into the Pacific to protect our ships
from British whaling ships with letters of marque attacking
ours. She did well until her capture off the Chile coast.
William Manning, Nathaniel Hawthorne's uncle, had shares
in 17 ships through 1812-1814. He sailed himself aboard
the sloop Hunter, the brig Rover, and the brig Neutrality
as captain. The schooner Fame, which a replica sails from
the harbor today, was a fishing boat that carried 2 guns
and 30 men. She was owned by John Becket Jr., William
Webb, Holten J. Breed, Henry Gordon, Pillet Allen, Jed
Upton, Lewis Folsom, John Clarke, Benjamin Upton,
James Cheever Jr., John Sage, Asa Reeves, Emery Johnson,
Enoch Manning, Charles Vandeford, John Brown, Daniel
Brookhouse, John Derby the 4th, Benjamin Chapman,
Benjamin Daniel's, Stephen Burchmore, John Sinclair,
Nathaniel Herd, George Leach, and James Brown. The Fame
was pink in color and sent the first prize into Salem. She
was captained by William Webb . Then Captain Green sailed
her out and captured five ships in fifteen days and sailed
them into Boston. The John captained by J. Crowninshield

had 16 guns and 100 men captured 11 vessels in 3 weeks. The John was soon to be captured early in the war though. His other ship Diomede had 16 guns and 104 men that took 10 vessels before she was captured in 1814. The Alexander was an 18 gun ship with 127 men captained by Benjamin Crowninshield. She took 7 prizes before she was run aground and taken. The Frolic captained by Odiorne burned 9 of its prizes at sea and fitted the other two with the prisoners to sail to England. In total Salem sent out 40 ships with 189 guns and 2,142 sailors. 250 ships were commissioned nationally for the War of 1812. By the close of 1813 the receipts from the sales of prizes brought into Salem was $675,695.93.

There was a shipping blockade created by the British, but New England states were issued licenses to continue shipping by British Admiral John Borlase Warren. In some cases New England merchants set up deals with British officers to have their ships captured with the cargo they were selling to support England's effort to fight Napoleon in Spain. This blockade resulted in a decrease of exports from $130 million in 1807 to $7 million in 1814. Salem faired well because the Orient Trade was kept open. Now American Privateers captured 1,300 prizes with the Navy only capturing 224 British ships. However Lloyd's of London reported only 1,175 British ships were taken with 373 returned. The British captured 1,593 ships from the Great Lakes to the West Indies. The War of 1812 was the last time the British used privateers and created the fall of the Bermuda's privateering pirates.

The end of the war came with the Treaty of Ghent in Belgium in 1814. The blockade of the American coast had hindered British interest in the West Indies and Canada that depended on the New England trade. Also privateering was proving troublesome to the British through higher insurance rates. Also British landowners had enough of high taxes. Plus those who had colonial interests and mercantile interest with America called for the trade to reopen by ending the war.

In 1815 came about the Second Barbary War where with the Napoleonic War and the War of 1812 over the superior ships of Netherlands, England, and America brought an end to the Muslim pirates. In 1816 Madison created the Second Bank of the United States after removal of factions in the Federalist Party was going to use it for their own benefit . Madison also learned it would have been useful during the War to support a standing army and curb inflation. The country was in the Era of Good Felling now.

James Monroe won easily against a Federalist Party in disarray after their lack of support for the War of 1812. He led a tour through the country in 1817 and won over the remaining Federalists. In July president Monroe visited Salem. He opened Old Town Hall, visited Stephen White in his home on the common, attended another ball in Mr. White's brother-in-law's, Judge Joseph Story, home on Winter Street, and stayed at his Secretary of the Navy's home on Derby Street which is now the Brookhouse Home for Aged Women. All of these building's he visited were once connected to the smuggler's tunnels in Salem. Monroe came again in 1819 and visited Senator Nathaniel Silsbee on the common in the building which is now the Knights of Columbus which also had tunnels running through it. In fact by his second election 1820 he ran unopposed. In turn since there was no opposition the Democratic-Repulican Party almost disappeared. Monroe with Henry Clay, and Andrew

Jackson granted $1000,000 for the African Colonization Society in 1816 to prevent several thousand freed slaves from revolting in the south and created the country Liberia. Its capital Monrovia was named after Monroe. Between 1820 to 1840 freed slaves left the country for Liberia.

The year 1825 brought John Quincy Adams to the presidency. The same year he dines with the Salem East India Marine Society. Here is a brief overview of his political history. In April 1802 Adams runs for Massachusetts State Senate and wins. Then in November he lost his bid for the U.S. House of Representatives running as a Federalist. Latter in 1803 he is elected to U.S. senate and remains till 1808. His support for Louisiana Purchase and the Embargo Act lost him the favor of the Federalists. He broke with the party and resigned his seat on Jun. 8th of 1808. Madison appointed him Minister to Russia where he seen Napoleon's invasion of Russia in 1812 nd his retreat in 1814. He was then sent to Ghent, Belgium to negotiate the end of the War of 1812. He served as Secretary of State as a Democratic-Republican under Monroe from 1817-1825 in which he helped in the purchase of Florida and the writing of the Monroe Doctrine. In 1824 the First Party System had eroded with the disappearance of the Democratic-Republican and the Federalist parties. In 1824 variety of local parties emerged throughout the nation with their own candidates. Andrew Jackson won the popular vote but did not have enough of a majority to win the electoral vote. So the house of Representatives elected John Quincy Adams after Henry Clay stepped down and became his Secretary of State. The feeling that the campaign was rigged which hindered his presidency and ultimately led to his loss to Jackson in the next election. At which time he ran for U.S. House of Representatives in 1830 as a National Republican.

He was elected for 17 years until his death in 1848. In 1836 he became a Whig. In 1834 he ran as an Anti-Masonic candidate for Ma. Governor and lost.

John Quincy Adams frequented Salem often since his first cousin was married to Joseph Barlow Felt . This house is now the residence of patrons visiting the Peabody Essex Museum who have donated over $1 million dollars. Now Joseph Barlow Felt had owned the Fame with Joseph White and Joseph White Jr., in 1804. They sell it to Joseph J. Knapp in 1805 who masters it himself and has it captured at St. Pierre in the West Indies in 1825. Also John Quincy was married to George Crowninshield Sr.. grand Niece. In 1825 he dined with the Salem East India Marine Society who founded the Museum. In fact he delivered the opening address of the East India Marine Hall of the Peabody Essex Museum on Oct. 14th of that year presided by Hon. Stephen White. After his presidency he gave a speech at the Salem Lyceum Society circa. 1831 on faith and government. The Salem Lyceum Society in future years would be a venue for abolitionist in future, a move John Quincy would approve of since he tried passing many reforms through congress to limited slavery calling it an evil feature of society as a whole. He will also be present with Superior Court Justice Joseph story in the Armistad case.

Murder. Captain Joseph White in his 82nd year is stabbed and bludgeoned to death in his sleep. Deep fear sets into the Salem Brahmins. Murder has struck down one of their own. This will become one of the most talked about cases in the early history of American law. Also it will prompt the local Parker Brothers to buy the U.S. Rights to Cluedo an English game that they renamed Clue. This would be Daniel Webster's most controversial case.

Daniel Webster was a prominent lawyer and statesman. At the end of his 2nd stint in office he did not seek a third term in the house and went back to his legal career in 1817. He went on to argue 223 cases in the Supreme Court and won half of them. Lot of these cases he took part in helped interpret the boundaries of the Constitution which gave him the name the Great Expounder of the Constitution. Through Salem he met Associate Justice Joseph Story of Salem and later these families will be bonded by marriage.

Judge Joseph story had once said of Webster "He was known as a lawyer; but he has now secured the title of an eminent and enlightened statesman." at the time Webster was elected to be a delegate from Massachusetts in 1820. In 1822 he was elected to the House again. In 1827 he was elected to Senate. He resisted the tariffs of 1816 and 1824 for the Federalists because they sponsored the manufacturing base in the country opposed to the shipping interest who was buying foreign manufactures. Then with his new friends the Lawrences and Lowells who opened mills in the towns respectfully named after them he supported the 1828 tariff.

In 1830 Salem's first privateer and partner with the Cabot brothers in Beverly was murdered in his home. This home was connected to the smuggling tunnels in Salem. The man who thought that any man could be sold into slavery for a price has been killed in his sleep. He had retired from the sea sometime before 1800 but still owned several ships. Captain White lived in the house with his niece Mrs. Mary Beckford, his housekeeper, Lydia Kimball, maid-of-all-work, and Benjamin White, who did odd jobs and was a distant relative. Mrs. Beckford's daughter had lived in the home for several years and Captain White was very fond of her until... Mary White Beckford fell in love with Joseph Jenkins Knapp, Jr. who was employed on one of Captain White's ships. Captain White forbid the relationship and fired Knapp and wrote marry out of the will when they married in 1827. In 1830 they were living on her mother's farm that Captain White gave her in Wenham.

The Knapps were a well respected family involved in shipping and mercantilism. They had several favorable dealings with Captain White. Captain Joseph Jenkins Knapp Sr.. bought the Revenge from White in 1805 which he will have confiscated by foreign powers. He was part owner with Joseph Barlow Felt, who married John Quincy Adam's cousin, of the Revenge. Joseph Jenkins Knapp was born that year. His brother Nathaniel Phippen was born in 1806 with John Francis in 1810. By the time Joseph Jenkins Knappp Jr. was 20 he was the captain of the Governor Wilson for his father and at 21 captained the Caroline for Joseph White. In 1825 he was admitted to the Salem East India Marine Society.

Now John Francis Knapp, or Frank, met George and "Dick" Crowninshield before he was 17 when they robed their father Richard Crowninshield Sr.., brother to Secretary of the Navy Benjamin Crowninshield, of $300 to go to New York. There they lived on petty thievery before they were caught and went to jail. Upon release Gorge sailed to New Orleans, "Dick" almost married the daughter of a wealthy plantation owner in Charleston, and Frank was forgiven when he got home and was sent to sea. In 1830 Frank was back and unemployed for several months. Now Nathaniel Phippen Knapp, who was known as Phippen, graduated from Harvard and passed the Bar right before

Captain White's death.

Richard Crowninshield Sr. was Benjamin Crowninshield's brother who married poorly to an Irish immigrant who was working as a maid in a New York hotel. She had a mean temper and was much in the gossip of Salem. In 1804 his first son Richard was born and their third son George in 1806. Richard Crowninshield Sr.. was part owner of the ship Romp which was confiscated by the French in Naples. His other partners were Joseph J. Knapp, Nathaniel Silsbee, and Joseph White Jr. . Part of the confiscation was the White Brothers ship Sukey & Betsey. Was there an altercation between the Crowninshields and the Whites over the matter. Later the Whites brother-in-law Judge Story would usurp his former employers, Crowninshields, in Congress.

April 7th of 1830 Benjamin White found Captain Joseph White dead in his bed. Nothing was stolen from his house but he lay there dead. 2,000 of Salem citizens went to Old Town Hall to find out what to do next. A committee of vigilance was created among 27 men with the power to search every house and interrogate every individual touching the murder. The group met at Stephen White's house nightly on the Commons and was given $1,000 and sworn to secrecy. Strangely enough Stephen hired no detectives nor informed the Sheriff. When Judge Story heard about the murder he grabbed Stephen by the collar and shook him violently accusing him. The town armed themselves with pistols, cutlasses, and watch dogs as they kept busy carpenters and smiths fixing bolts to doors and fastenings to windows thinking they would be next.

Stephen White was the son of Captain Henry White (dead in 1824) who was Captain Joseph White's brother.

Stephen's brother was Joseph "Junior" White. They lived
next to each other in mansions on the commons connected
to their uncle's home by means of tunnels. They had a third
brother named Francis. Their homes were connected to
Stephen's brother-in-law's house, Judge Joseph Story. The
brothers Joseph "Junior" and Stephen were bankrolled
by their uncle Captain Joseph White and created the
commercial house Joseph Jr. & Stephen White. In 1807
as the Embargo Act engaged Joseph "Junior" White met
Judge Story and married his sister in 1808. At the wedding
Stephen announced his engagement to the other Story
daughter. Joseph White Jr. and Joseph Story were both
state representatives. April 1807 Congressman Jacob
Crowninshield spat up blood while speaking in Congress
and soon died. Story was the Crowninshield family lawyer.
Benjamin Crowninshield was tapped to replace his brother
but Story helped push forth by the White brothers took his
seat and removed the power from the Crowninshield family.
Story lobbied for Jefferson's downfall after the Embargo
Act and became the Federalist's favorite Democratic-
Republican. Power in Salem was now in the hands of the
White family and the Story's. They would start the Friday
Evening Club, which brought together 10 members being
friends and family of Story, that would discuss affairs of
banks, insurance companies, and the local Democratic-
Republican Party. Was the instigation of the George and
"Dick" Crowninshield in the future murder of the elderly
Captain Joseph White meant to be a final nail in the
Crowninshield power by Story?

In 1815 Joseph Jr. & Stephen White took up selling
opium from Turkey to China and Indonesia. Joseph Peabody
was the leading dealer of opium at the time. Also in 1817
they made huge profits in the Falklands killing baby Seals.

Stephen White also incorporates the East India Marine Hall Corporation to cover liabilities of the new home for the museum in 1824. The Salem East India Marine Society is largest investor. On the first floor of the bank Stephen opened the Asiatic Bank and Oriental Insurance Company. Joseph Ropes and Tucker Daland resigned from the Merchants Bank. Robert Stone who was Stephen uncle resigned from the Commercial Bank. They all joined Stephen's new bank. In 1827 Captain Joseph J. Knapp Jr. worried Stephen by not keeping proper contact with him. What confounded the issue was Stephen' wife and mother dies that year. The brunt of this would be taken out on Joseph J. Knapp Jr. when he returns to Salem. This would be the last ship he would ever sail for Stephen. To further his ire he would mary his cousin Mary Beckford.

Joseph "Junior" White had died in 1819 and his wife Eliza or Betsy, Judge Story's sister, lived in the home up to 1831 when she sold it to the Silsbee family. He had left three daughters. Stephen was married to Harriet Story who also gave him 3 daughters. One of them married Daniel Webster's son Col. Daniel Fletcher Webster. Stephen was elected several times to both branches of legislature. Stephen inherits $250,000 from his uncle on his death. Six of Judge Story's nieces receive $25,000 a piece. Captain Joseph White's will was changed right before his death.

From testimonies that Stephen White gathered from a conversation 3 years ago from people who still sat in jail that in "Dick" Crowninshield's gambling hall they heard him and George Crowninshield plan to steal Captain White's iron chest. At the murder which happened 3 years later, nothing was stolen. From 6 P.M. to 4 A.M. on the morning of the murder mysterious people have been seen on Brown

Street behind Captain Joseph White's home on Essex Street. On April 27th Joe and Frank Knapp were attacked in their carriage returning from Salem to Wenham. On May 2nd the committee of vigilance arrested "Dick" and George along with Benjamin Selman and David Chase. A grand jury in Ipswich charged "Dick" with murder and the rest as being present, aiding, and abetting the murder. Selman and Chase was in Salem that night with no proof "Dick" was. Selman and Chase were in the gambling hall 3 years ago with "Dick" when the allegations were heard. The Newburyport Herald reported "that the efforts of the committee in Salem can hardly be overpraised".

On May 14th Captain Joseph Jenkins Knapp Sr.. received a letter from Belfast Maine accusing him of some transaction he sent his brother Franklin to do on 2nd of April last which he paid too much for. The black mailer got the father mistaken for his son Joseph Jr. The next day the father went to Wenham to ask his sons Joseph and Frank. They told him they should present it to the Committee of Vigilance. Two other letters were sent. One to the chairman of the Committee of Vigilance Dr. Gideon Barstow and the other to Stephen White both accusing Stephen of the murder and not paying the black mailer the $5,000 he promised. So at a meeting at Stephen White's house they decided to only investigate the Knapp letter...

They sent attorney Joseph Waters to search out the black mailer. He found John C. R. Palmer who was 23 years old. He was brought to Salem in chains and brought about the arrest of the Knapp brothers. A friend of Stephen White, Rev. Henry Colman, visited the brothers in jail. Colman performed Joseph's marriage. Colman was a man of violent temper. From his visits to their cells he became the star witness for the prosecution of the Knapp brothers. Also it was Colman who some how had divine intervention to look in the Howard Street meeting house to find a club under the stairs. The Knapp brothers are tricked into confessions that contradict each other as their brother Phippen the lawyer is barred from seeing them.

"Dick" was sitting in jail reading, visiting with friends, writing verse, and learning math and mechanics. Very well calmed. It was said after a conversation with the Knapp's defense attorney this pimp and gambler believed if he was dead they could not try the rest. So "Dick" was found hanging by two silk handkerchiefs from the cell window with his legs bent and his knees a foot from the floor. This was taken as proof of his guilt?

On July 10th the attorney general, solicitor general, and 4 of the justices of the Supreme Judicial Court were in Salem; Chief Justice Isaac Parker, Associate Justice Samuel Putnam, Associate Justice Samuel Summer Wilde, and Associate Justice Marcus Morton. Selman and Chase were let free and the Knapps and Crowninshields were indicted. Their attorney was Franklin Dexter who defended a man who was said to libel Daniel Webster. On July 27th Chief Justice Parker is dead. On July 30th Webster takes the case for his friends Judge Joseph Story and Stephen White.

It came out from the coroner report that he was stabbed with a Dirk 13 times but loss no blood because of the blow to his head that occurred first (In my opinion, I think I heard that if a body is stabbed after it is dead it does not bleed?). That Benjamin Leighton was napping on the farm and overheard the Knapp brothers complaining that "Dick" was taking too long to kill Captain White. After a mistrial

and Lorenzo Knapp's story in the paper the jury was riveted
by Webster's closing arguments and had Frank hanged
with his brother following him soon afterwards. George
Crowninshield was proven to be in bed with two ladies on
the night of the murder and was set free.

So what do you think? Did they get the right person for
the murder? Why did they keep the tunnels secret? What
would of happened if Joseph Jenkins Knapp Sr.. had the
political ties that Stephen White had? Why were they so set
on "Dick" instead of George being the murderer? What do
you think? Did it stir your imagination? It stirred Edgar Alan
Poe to write his story "The Tell Tale Heart" though! It even
stirred Howard Bradley in 1956 when they published a book
on Webster when they found people in Salem who viewed
inquiries into the case with alarm over a 100 years later...

This murder and the advent of the clipper ship had
brought an end to the wealth in Salem by the 1850's.
Enterprise had turned to Naumkeag Mills and the tanneries
on the North River. The tunnels continue to stretch down
Boston Street through Beaver Street to the tanneries on the
North River. Alas this is a subject for the sequel to this book
detailing the tunnel system from North Street and beyond
into the McIntire District.

Then in 1838 we have a hero. The son of a naturalized
citizen from Curacao off the Venezuelan coast,
Charles Lenox Remond was elected to be one of the agents
of the Massachusetts Anti-Slavery Society. Remond was
from the same tribe that Tituba was said to be from, the
Arawak. His family owned hair salons, whig shops,
saloons, and catering companies. His father John had ran
a catering company out of Hamilton Hall. Charles' sister

Sarah Parker Remond was also an abolition activist who shared the stage with Susan B. Anthony. These two caught the attention of Fredrick Douglass who had lived in Lynn for a period of time. The three would share the stage and give lectures. Fredrick respected Charles so much he named his first child Charles Lenox Douglass after him. The two did differ on the recruitment of the famed 54th and 55th Massachusetts Infantry that appear in the movie Glory. Fredrick was a pacifist. Most likely he used the tunnels under Hamilton Hall to move slaves in the Underground Railroad.

Other houses said to be connected to the Underground Railroad by the smuggling tunnels are the house which sits at 4 Beacon Street now, the House of Seven Gables, and the Downing Block which houses Gene Murray' Dance Studio. The Downing Block has many compartments in its basement attached to the tunnel which have been said to quarter runaway slaves.

Daniel Webster supported the Fugitive Law of 1850 that required federal officials to recapture and return runaway slaves. Horace Mann denounced him as "a fallen star! Lucifer descending from Heaven!" James Russell Lowell called him the " most meanly and foolishly treacherous man I ever heard.". He tried to persecute those who freed Shadrack Minkins from Boston officials bent on returning him to his owner and lost. When Webster warned the anti-slavery Liberty Party would enforce the Fugitive Law they freed William Henry who was a Syracuse resident which was being shipped back to Missouri where he escaped from in spite of his threat. In 1852 he lost his presidency attempt and died that year of cirrhosis of the liver from years of drinking. "Black Dan" had many mistresses, drank heavy, spent more than he had, and gambled a lot. I wonder if Webster owed "Dick" Crowninshield a large gambling debt?

To Webster's chagrin in 1920 prohibition began and ran till 1933. Abstinence societies like the "Cork Total Abstinence Society" was founded in the 1800's. The founder Father Theobald Matthew came to the U.S. in 1849 to start a 2 year tour across the country. He came to Salem on Sept. 19, 1849. His statue was originally on Central Street next to a distilery that opened in 1772 which is now Murphy's Bar (Roosevelt's). This spot was originally the site of one of the town wells that was polluted by the city's sewage system. The statue was dedicated in 1887. The Gideon Tucker house was remolded in 1910 by the Total Abstinence Society. There was other groups in town like the Young Men's Catholic Temperance Societies (1843), Washington Total Abstinence Union and Martha Washington Society (1841-1847), Henfield Division, Sons of Temperance (1844), Salem Division (1846), Young Men's Division (1859-1865), Phillip's Division (1859), Abraham Lincoln Division (1866), Independent Division, Daughters of Temperance, and Zephyr Union Daughters, Social Council (1859), Essex Temple Honor (1856), Meteoric Temple for Honor (1866), Cadets of Temperance (1848), and 14 others I do not feel writing. So at least these groups were happy when prohibition came along.

The rest turned to the smuggling tunnels again to transport and travel through to the local speakeasies. In Salem they were called "Bungholes". In fact the Bunghole on Derby Street used to have one of these establishments where their storage room is now connected by the tunnels. Most taverns on Derby Street were connected to these tunnels plus the various distilleries on that road. The Sun

Tavern where the Bowker Block now stands has tunnels in which the Peabody Essex Museum still uses to access the office building. John Stone, Amos Gile, Captain Jonathan Hodges Jr., and Col Pearce were distillers in town. Before the smugglers had to sneak in the molasses and sugar to make rum, now they had to sneak out the liquor. The world was turned on its ear in Salem, but the tunnels still proved useful to this generation.

Now the women could turn to Lydia Pinkham and her "Vegetable Compound- a positive cure for all those Complaints and Weakness so common to our female population" During prohibition this cure had 18% alcohol. Life Magazine in 1949 said that 2 or 3 bottles taken at once would help any woman forget her problems and her Christian name. One of Pinkham adds ran "A fearful Tragedy-Clergyman of Stratford, Conn. KILLED BY HIS OWN WIFE-Insanity Brought on by 16 Years of Suffering With_FEMALE COMPLAINTS the CAUSE-Lydia Pinkham's Vegetable Compound-The Sure Cure for These Complaints. Its most successful history was during the 20's and 30's and had seen sales decline after prohibition. Now in 1922 Lydia's daughter opened a women's clinic named after her, right next to where the Theobald Matthew statue was moved to on opposite corners of Hawthorne Blvd. and New Derby Street.

So how were the tunnels used in our generation? Daniel Low started his company in 1867 which converted a stretch of the tunnels to move cargo from his warehouse to the store which his company still used up to the 90's. In the 50's there still could be tunnels leading to brothels on Derby Street. Old men remember rowing into the tunnels of the South River under the Wendy's on Lafayette Street. Some

years ago a child got lost in them. Until recently I heard
of stories of during a night of drinking a group went to
venture into the tunnels in the Hodges House on Orange and
Essex and turned around because it was flooded and had too
many rats. People have seen them expose the roof of this
tunnel when digging in the yard. My friends at 24 Lynde
Street would walk a little ways into them under the house.
The Black Cat Book store on Essex Street where Sylvia's
mediumship parlor called Past, Present, Future is now had
access too. In the 80's Chuck's Steak House took 12 feet of
the tunnel in the Derby Pickman building next to Old Town
Hall and converted it into a wine cellar. Thomas Mackey
has stories to tell of the tunnels he has worked in fixing the
utilities under the road for years. A construction crew few
years ago called the city engineers when they discovered
the roof of the tunnels in the alley of City hall. A telephone
repairman friend of mine in the 70's had seen the tunnels
in the 7 Gables and under Red Lion Smoke Shop that enter
into the sealed off track of the train tunnel under Washington
Street. Prisoners were rumored to leave the Salem Jail by
tunnel for conjugal visits at home and would come back
by Monday. Friends of mine used to play in the tunnels
attached to the Judge Story House on Winter Street. Another
friend played in the tunnels under her grandmother's house
on Boston Street. A friend worked for the Registry of Deeds
when it was on Federal Street and talked about the tunnels
that led from there to the court house on the corner of
Washington Street. Also this tunnel had a separate train stop
for the Judges and under the Superior Court is a room filled
with photographs of all the murders that happened in the
county since the 1800's.

How else have they been used? Why are they still secret.
Ask a utility worker, as they are plentiful digging into these

old tunnels at the time I am writing this in 2011, if they exist he will say no. They have police details who look at you funny if you stand too long looking into them. I have been able to get some pictures of the old tunnels in the road and been yelled at by an angry midget with a hard hat on. The police deny it, but old city engineers love to talk about them. The Peabody Essex Museum is still connected in more than one way. Descendants hate to talk about anything from the past either it be the Witch Craft Trials to the ancient smuggling that went on. Could these tunnels have been still used during the 80's to move drugs from the sea to their final destinations? Could we have tours through them or find them on the Discovery Channel one day? These questions still need to be answered?

Preface:

Well I have heard stories about the tunnels ever since I moved here in 1992. I have come close to them many times, but never pursued them. I have been in a book store years ago that was connected to them, but never asked to venture in them. I have been in a girlfriend's house and starred at a wine cellar and did not know it was part of the tunnel. I worked for a ghost tour and walked through another part of them, but did not dare walk past the fire door that rolled into the wall. I learned after the fact I used to visit friends in an apartment they rented that allowed them to walk through the tunnels. Like most I was fascinated with the stories of the tunnels, but never realized they were under my nose or dreamed of the extent of them. Even after walking through a section of the tunnels my brain still pushed them into the category of myth.

Maybe that is what is so fun about them, they fit a place in the world shrouded by myth and lore. Like all the good content of a fairy tale represents what lies below your conscious mind the tunnels lies just outside of your reason under your feet. Just a few feet below almost anywhere you walk within the downtown of Salem they are there. In scale to how deep you must scale down into your subconscious mind to access the images of your dreams, resentments, wishes, your shortcomings, fears, and your greatest potential are how far the roofs of these tunnels are to your shoes.

In a way to go beyond the threshold blocked by the police patrolling the entrances of these old tunnels as utility workers are walking through them to take a good look is the first step into yourself. To walk through them is crossing that threshold into the journey of the hero. There is an adrenaline that pierces your heart and mind as you walk through the darkness of these tunnels. You have entered the land of myth and lore where captains ordered sailors and smugglers alike to move mysterious cargo from the orient through these chambers. A place where gold flowed freely filled with rum and vice. A journey through time where you might bump into a man off to visit a mistress, a gentlemen eluding complications that may arise from his presence in a brothel, a young man's life who is about to change for the worse as he is being led unconscious out to sea. A land shrouded in a time of heros like Fredrick Douglass and Charles Lenox Remond moving runaway slaves to freedom. In keeping a fascination for these tunnels you are keeping that miraculous place within you alive.

Now how can you help me find them all? Let me tell you what I know about the tunnels. Elias Hasket Derby Jr. has come back from a successful journey from sea that landed him a fortune in 1791. His father dies in 1799 leaving him a large money pit on the site where Old Town Hall is now. By 1801 the town is split between Federalist and Democratic-Republicans. Jefferson is calling for high duties to be paid to the Customs House in lieu of high tariffs. That year Derby takes over the Second Corp of Cadets and positions them in the Franklin Building (Present site of the Hawthorne Hotel in which their clubhouse still sits upon) in which his group the Salem Marine Society owns. He has these men tear down the hills in the commons and fills in the ponds. In the process he is creating a place to smuggle all of the dirt into from a new leg of tunnel digging.

He has learned from his grandfather in building the brick house on Derby Street that you need a bigger home and to build it quicker to avoid any questions that might alert someone to the tunnels you are building. When you have a pile of bricks three times the size of the finished house you intend to build, people will rightly ask where are all of the bricks going? Brick yards might raise an eyebrow when you tell them you plan to build only one home. So Elias Jr. had planned to expand on the tunnel that led from his wharf through the brick house to that of his cousins the Hodges on the corner of Orange and Essex Streets. That distance between the brick Derby house and that of Benjamin Hodges (another member of the Salem East India Marine Society) was going to be the new increment to measure the amount of bricks you can hide with the erection of two 3 story brick Federal Style mansions being built simultaneously next to each other. Derby surmised that the best mason could not estimate the correct amount of bricks it would take to build such homes at a glance. So after Derby had graded the common, planted trees, and surrounded the commons with a wooden fence he inspired the network of captains who has worked for his family to move and construct new homes around this common. These homes would be spaced the distance of the length of Orange Street (the same distance from the Derby's brick house to the Hodges Home) and would have two 3 story brick Federal Style homes built next to each other. If these homes were built on a cross road they might build 3 of these homes next to each other to accommodate the amount of bricks for the split in the tunnel. Each of these homes would at least have 4 exterior chimneys.

Why? Why 4 exterior chimneys? You might not ask
that today since most homes built with chimneys are built
outside of the house. You might also wonder why fireplaces
are uneconomical to heat your home with? In the time
before and after the construction of these homes they knew
that a central fireplace and chimney with all four sides
enclosed within your home would most effectively preserve
the heat within the house. If you asked these captains
and merchants why they wasted having 4 faces of their
chimneys exposed to the exterior they might tell you they
have so much money they could afford the waste. On the
other hand they are fighting so the rest of the country pays
higher tariffs and they would not have to pay duties on any
of their cargo. Also they are fighting with the town assessors
office that the half floor above the second should not be
taxed as a whole floor. So they are very conscious of every
dime, so why waste energy with these exterior chimneys?

They needed one line of tunnels to move cargo to
underground warehouses, banks, and stores while the
other line of tunnel could have the empty carts return
unobstructed. Now below these grand fireplaces placed on
the four corners of the homes are support arches that stretch
at least 4 feet into the basement. Now you can join the
tunnel to these homes with a weather tight seal if the doors
are inside the basement. Also these arches had holes leading
up through the fireplaces above and out the chimneys which
could draw in air from various manholes throughout town.
Some of the houses have a second or third chimney in line
which each other that bisects the other four in the center of
the house. These chimneys show you from above when the
tunnel would have followed a second course. These homes
sit on a subterranean crosSr.oad. So as you look for homes
that could possibly be connected to the tunnels look in the

sky and line up the chimneys. Also look for homes that are set back from the sidewalk in line of these chimneys. These houses are set back because they were persuaded by the smugglers not to dig their foundations into the middle of their tunnels.

Now the nineteenth century in Salem there was great public work projects to fill in the various coves and rivers in town. As the wagons filled with dirt were moving down from the Highlands off Marlboro Road it was easy to sneak in a wagon or two of dirt from the tunnels being dug throughout town. They filled in and extended Beacon Street, Barton Street, Webb Street, Milk Street, Briggs Street, Collins Cove, Forester Street, Boardman Street, New Derby Street, the South River, the current train station, and Canal Street to name a few. The fountain in front of the East India Mall is a sculpture of Salem representing the old coastline in the raised section and the current coastline in the recessed section.

The old tunnels and the ones that connect to the stores on Essex Street have different entrances. Some of these have ones very similar to the ones under the fireplace arches with no chimneys above them. Others just show blocked off doorways. A few of these entrances still have doors into the tunnels. You can find these by looking for an area of brick that is different or have been made of newer material. Sometimes these portals would have holes in the floors in front of them. In these holes variously covered are sewage lines that come up from the tunnels. At some point in our history they converted the tunnels into being corridors to lay utilities in. Why dig a new hole? Also why dig a new hole into these buildings when you can use a pre-existing one. So when you venture into these basements you can find where the tunnel entrances were by finding the sewage pipes in the floor. Some of these holes are wide enough for a ladder to fit down into. Depending on the various grades throughout town some of the houses had to enter the tunnels through trapdoors.

So that leads us to another set of markers in town. Follow the path of manhole covers marked by "S", Drain, Sewer, and "SELCO". These manholes lead pass the Downing Block, Derby-Pickman Block, Old Town Hall, down from the Armory to New Derby Street, Up Pleasant Street to Collins Street, and beyond. In fact the tunnel at 4 Beacon Street leads from the back of the house to the last manhole on Barton Street. There are also square open faced utility conduit openings that can be seen in front of the Hawthorne Hotel on Essex Street, The Lawrence Block on Front Street, and the Armory to name a few places. These were used as dog legs set at fixed distances to allow one crew push a cart of cargo to give way to another. All of these places were once connected by tunnels. Also you can see glass brick in the sidewalk that was put there so you can see your keys as you tried to enter the buildings from the tunnels. The best example can be seen in front of the Gulu-Gulu on Essex Street next to the bench. In the planter outside what is now the Gathering Church toward the back on Derby Square you can see the pavement they used to cover the glass brick you can see from inside the tunnel. On the corner off of Essex Street where there is a concrete slab to hold a bench is another. Below the slab is a series of glass panes used to illuminate a basement office that extended into the tunnel on two sides. In fact around the corner below the bricks is another row of glass panes. The rest of the face of the building has corrugated steel holding up the sidewalk. There is also a concrete lined shaft with a square iron top in front

of the Knights of Columbus in the Commons. In front of
the White-Hodges house on the corner of Winter Street and
Washington Square is another square lid you can enter by
prying it with an old brake shoe someone left there years
ago.

Another marker is when you see stretches of lawn that
look like giant gophers have burrowed through them. As
you can see with the erosion exposing the bricks on top
of the tunnels at Fort Pickering on Winter Island that they
are domed. So the lawns behind the Derby House and the
Customs House have a domed shape to them. Also a line
leads from the tomb doors facing Bridge Street running
parallel to Howard street in the cemetery sharing the same
name. This raised line runs to the old school and then takes
a left towards the street. Gravestones only mark the bottom
of the mound on the left and point towards the bodies being
buried extended away from the mound. Then tombs line the
top on the right. There are no bodies buried in the mound.
Also you can see this mound shape on Essex Street as the
cobblestones are sinking into the ground. Then never walk
down the public road leading to the Cabot Farm or you
might wake up the guard roosters. Then someone goes up
and down the street after they call the police. See the Cabot
Farm stretches down to the river and has a tunnel running
from under the chapel in the Green Lawn Cemetery to their
homes. The road is badly humped and terminates into the
field where it splits into two tunnels leading to their homes.
In the field the tunnels create two passes that remain high
and dry with puddles forming to either side. The homes
are said to have many secret passages as well. The Cabots
were the first privateers along with Captain White. Plus they
were the countries second and third millionaires. So I did
mention the tunnels under the chapel?

Now we come to the deduction you can only gain from books. On Google Books there are many texts you can access on Salem's History which give details on the history of the various houses and the people who built them. From these observations I found that those related to Derby, Crowninshield, and Hodges or have worked for these families in some capacity had built these homes or stores. They used the same architects or masons. They are built by Samuel McIntire, Samuel Field McIntire, Joseph McIntire, William Roberts, Joushua Upham, and David Lord. It was amusing to see a variety of people who have tunnels connected to their homes pay all of these masons to build the Customs House on Derby Street on the old Crowninshield homestead.

As to the veracity of my conjectures and facts I will tell you which houses I have been in and show you photos of the tunnels or their sealed entrances and which ones are conjectures. Also I am easy to reach if you have access or a story to a house where the tunnels are, please do so.

So the rest of the book will talk about these families and the people in their employment. I will break down areas of the town into easy chunks so you could walk in an afternoon to see these houses that they built, one section at a time. You can enter the journey and fill your imagination of all the exploits that could of or did happen under your feet. Imagine the Salem East India Marine Society. They were an elite group of Federalists that had amongst several objectives to bring curiosities back from the Orient and beyond. It must of been OK to travel above ground with teapots, Samurai swords, and cannibal forks, but if you are moving the Romanov crown jewels, an ancient library, Rosebud, religious artifacts, gold, silver, magical items, stolen art, and the like you would use the tunnels into the various basements and subbasements they own in town into their elaborate vaults. Things we will never see. You will learn the history of the houses and the neighborhood they resided in and lots more.

Also you will learn the history of these people and how they affected the early development of our country. How the mercantile, that is the equivalent of our big business, used their influence with their lobbyist, judges, statesmen, representatives,and senators to turn this government into what they wanted. You will follow along on maps in the book and maps on Google Maps accessible by Droid phones and any mobile device that can access the internet. You will see pictures of the houses, of the tunnels, and their entrances.

I will leave you with this thought.

If everyone runs a light at a 4 way stop no one gets through. If the majority abides the law and goes in their turn, traffic flows. But, even though the majority follows the law there is still a small fraction of people who can run that light on a constant basis without causing an accident interrupting the flow of traffic. Why let them....

Manhole covers to look for to follow the tunnel route through town.

Table of Contents

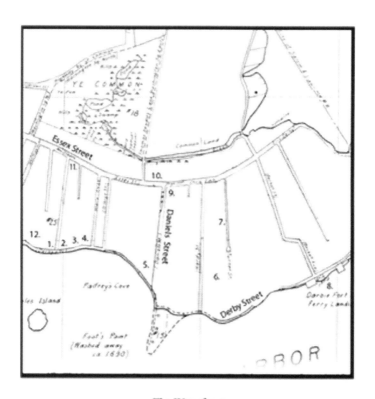

The Waterfront

Chapter 1

Waterfront

This section of our histories will start at the
Brookhouse for Aged Women which was originally
built for Benjamin Crowninshield. We will wind our
way down Derby Street to the Ferry and come back
upon ourselves and head up Daniel's Street to head
south on Essex and end at the Hawthorne Hotel.
This was the old waterfront district. Philips, Central,
Union, Pickering, and Derby wharves ran from the
coast. Here all of the goods were smuggled into the
wharfs before the customs agents could peer within
their ship holds. From the various wharfs goods were
smuggled through trap doors into the tunnels that led
to the merchants and ship captains homes. There the
goods were stored till they moved them to their stores
on Essex Street to sell. In some circumstances raw
goods were not only stored in these houses but were
transferred into sails, baked goods, rum, and clothing
which were then smuggled back onto the ships.

Also on the waterfront had seen its share of saloons
and brothels. Tunnels kept the gentlemen's privacy
intact when visiting the brothels and had ensconced
many men out to sea through Shanghai tunnels. The
neighborhood was split in two due to politics. To the
north was the Democratic-Republicans and to the
south was the Federalists. In the middle were the
Crowninshield and Derby families who sat on either
side of the fence who were intermarried in business
and the bedroom. Their goal was to split the town
down the middle and capitalize on both ends.

1. Benjamin Crowninshield Home
180 Derby Street at Orange

This house was built in 1810 for Benjamin Crowninshield
who served as Secretary of the Navy for Presidents Madison
and Monroe. The house was started by Samuel McIntire
and finished in 1811 after his death by his son Samuel
Field McIntire. In 1817 President Monroe stayed here
as he visited Salem on his tour through the country. This
was the first of several homes he wined and dined in that
was connected by the tunnels. So the question is, was he
oblivious of their existence or did he pass through them
to engagement to engagement. The Brookhouse for Aged
Woman bought it in 1860. Robert Brookhouse converted
the house by a fund raised mostly by subscription raised
in part by Rev. Michael Carlton of the Moral Society. The
Association for the Relief of Aged and Destitute Women

was incorporated from this subscription and the home reopened in 1861. The house is still open to this day. The tunnels run through the fireplace arches and lead to the Customs House on the way to the Hawkes and Derby house. Look up in the sky and see how the chimneys line up. Also you will notice the Simon Forester House is set back from the road to accommodate the passing of the tunnel under his lawn heading to the Richard Derby House next to the Bunghole.

Benjamin was one of the 4 brothers sired by George Crowninshield Sr.. .They were partners in Geo. Crowninshield & Sons who were a leading merchant family in Salem with several ships engaged mostly in the Pepper trade. By 1809 they had several wharves and 12 ships. They were staunch supporters of Jefferson and built their homes in he manor of the Federalists. They were bitter enemies of the Derby's even though their mother was Mary Derby. The Derby family were Federalists.

This reminds me of early Game Theory. You take over the two extremes and split the people down the middle and split the profits. In this way you eliminate the competition since the two parties pool their economic and political ties together to eliminate the competition. Much like Coke and Pepsi eliminated their competition in the 80's by having only taste challenges promoting each other. Their combined income on advertisement showcasing each other eliminated a slew of cola companies that existed prior. Another example is when two people are shipwrecked in a Banana Republic country in the novel Cat and the Cradle where the two friends splits the country in half. One becomes the religious leader leading the opposition against the other friend who becomes the dictator. Or how the world was split between Communism and Capitalism. Then in the 90's Yale Graduate John Kerry ran against John Edwards in the 2004 Democratic Primaries to loose to Yale graduate Republican incumbent president George W. Bush. This was following a principal of game theory established in Southampton University in England. They introduced a new strategy at the 20th-anniversary iterated prisoner's dilemma competition, which successful beat tit for tat. This strategy relied on cooperation between programs to achieve the highest number of points for a single side. Team A would work with Team B to defeat the rest of the teams. Team B would do its best to defeat everyone besides Team A. If the two teams of A and B entered the finals Team B would by default loose to Team A. Two people from Yale successfully entered the finals at the 2004 Presidential Race and Kerry lost by default. This was the first time since the Madison election that the Democrats and Republicans were once more the Democratic-Republican Party.

The Crowninshields and the Derbys split the town and the country down the middle. In 1757 Mary Derby, Elias Hasket's sister, marries George Crowninshield Sr.. in 1757. Elias Hasket Derby marries Elizabeth Crowninshield, George's sister, in 1761. George and Mary's daughter will marry Senator Nathaniel Silsbee. George also had a son named Jacob Crowninshield who brought the first live elephant to the United States in 1796. He purchased the two year-old female, which he described as "about the size of a very large ox", in India for $450 and sold her in New York City for $10,000. (The pachyderm toured the country as the "Crowninshield's Elephant" or "Stoned Elephant" until her final public exhibition in 1818. The elephant had a penchant for ale.). Later he turned down a position under Jefferson in 1805 to become the Secretary of the Navy in which his brother Benjamin accepted under Madison's term. He was Elected as a Republican to represent Massachusetts' 2nd District and as an At-Large in the Eighth and three terms in the U.S. Congresses, he served from 1803 until his death in office at the age of 38 in 1808. George Crowninshield Jr. took over Geo. Crowninshield & Co. on his father's death in 1815. He sailed the world in the countries first yacht The Cleopatra. His grand niece marries John Quincy Adams. George Crowninsheld Sr.. last son Richard would be the father of Richard ""Dick"" Crowninshield who hanged himself before he could be tried for the murder of Captain Joseph White.

Benjamin William Crowninshield also in 1811 became the president of the Merchant's Bank in the Brown Building across from the Hawthorne Hotel. Both buildings were connected to the tunnels. That same year he was elected to the Ma. House of Representatives and in 1812 to the Ma. Senate. During the War of 1812 one of his families privateer ships the "American" took 26 prizes on 4 journeys yielding $1 million. In 1815 he was appointed to Secretary of Navy and then served also under Monroe till he resigned in 1818 and went back to the Ma. House of Representatives. He was also the Collector of Customs for Marblehead. He dies in 1851.

2. Customs House
170 Derby Street at Orange Street

The current customs house was built in 1819 by plans
by Samuel McIntire after his death by Joseph McIntire
(his cousin), David Lord, Joshua Upham, and William
Roberts. It was built on property once owned by George
Crowninshield. George gained the property when he married
into the Derby family. The Crowninshield house looked
much like the Pickman-Derby-Brookhouse on Washington
Street (Current site of the Mason Lodge) that Elias Hasket
Derby lived in before he built his mansion in Derby Square.
Instead of having an eagle on top, it had a weather vane of a
merchant holding a spyglass.

   In 1819 the current customs house was selected for the
government by a commission headed by Joseph Story,

the Derby's, Joseph Peabody, and others to have their masons build it. All of these men have had tunnels built through their homes. Plus they chose the old Crowninshield homestead as the site for the new building. Where else would you build a tunnel for tax evasion than right under the Customs House. They had done the same thing when they built a tunnel under the Customs House at 6 Central Street which resided in the Central Building in 1805-1807 and then 1813-1819.

Previous to the customs house being here on Central Street it was across the street. The first customs house was called the "Port House" which was on the head of the South River. Another customs houses was on the corner of Gedney Court and Summer Street called the "French House" which later was the home of Judge Gedney. At this point in history the customs house was the private residence of the customs agent. Some of which lived in various boardinghouses at different times moving about quite regularly so the captains never knew where to find them when they have returned from sea if they ever did search for them. Then it was on Fort Ave by the Old Neck gate, then 154 Washington Street in the "Blaney Building", at 261 Essex Street, in 1776 on the corner of Essex and North, Opposite the Essex Institute on Essex Street, then the corner of Newbury and Essex Streets. There were 13 custom houses in Salem over the years. Now their offices are in the Cummings Center in Beverly.

As of yet I have not ventured into their basement. I can only conclude that there are tunnels leading from the warehouse in the back which does not have a corridor leading to the front where the offices are. The back yard is domed showing where the tunnel could lay. Plus the fact that the people who have their homes connected by tunnels in town chose this location and had their masons built it. In Salem when they build a new building on the site of an old home they keep the old foundation and expand it if necessary. So if the Crowninshield family seat had tunnels running through them I would assume the Customs House does too. Also part of the tunnel in front of the Customs House on the wharf caved in. Plus I have seen the tunnel leading into the old custom house in the Central Building on Central Street.

3. The Hawkes House
4 Customs House Court

Boat builder Benjamin Hawkes bought this home after Elias
Hasket Derby. Derby built it as his new mansion and never
moved in. He used it to store cargo he had accumulated
from his several privateers during the Revolutionary War.
Designed by Samuel McIntire in 1780. Derby moved into
the Pickman-Derby-Brookhouse house on Washington
instead in 1782 and left the house unfinished. The house
was then owned by Samuel Archer and Jonathan Mason.
Benjamin Hawkes and William B. Parker bought it in 1801
same year that his son Elias Hasket Derby Jr. starts digging
in the commons. In a deed dated in June 1801 Hawkes sells
the house to William B. Parker. Parker cuts his half of the
house off and then moves it off of Webb street.

I have not been able to venture into this basement as of yet.

4. The Derby House
168 Derby Street

This Georgian Colonial was built for Elias Hasket Derby
by his father Richard when he got married to Elizabeth
Crowninshield in 1762. The house was started in 1761 but
the roof was not put on till Jan 1762. Samuel McIntire's
father Joseph had built it. In 1778 they moved to the
Pickman-Derby-Brookhouse mansion on Washington Street
where the Mason lodge is now. In 1784 the Derby's ship
master Henry Prince buys the house and opens a storefront
in front of the home. Prince stopped going to see in 1805 to
settle down as a merchant. In 1811 Prince was forced to sell
the house to William Ropes after the Embargo Act ruined
him.

   The corner chimneys in the house line up with Hawkes
House and the Benjamin Crowninshield Home (Brookhouse

Home for Aged Women). There is an addition in the back with a separate chimney heading toward the Hodges home on Essex and Orange Streets. At this time I have not been able to get into the basements.

Richard Derby made his fortune at sea. He ran the blockades during the French and Indian War and outfitted his ships with many cannons. In fact he owned 8 of the 18 cannons that British General Leslie was order to confiscate prior to the Battle on the Green in Lexington. He yelled at General Leslie "Find the cannon if you can, take them if you can. They will never be surrendered.". His son John Derby would be the first to tell London the news of the Battle of Lexington. Then his first son Richard Derby Jr. was a strong political figure in Salem till his early death in 1781. Their father would die 2 years later.

Now Elias Hasket was the second son and most successful. He would become one of America's first millionaires along with the Cabots of Beverly. He would go on to outfit 158 vessels at sea during the Revolutionary War. He traded in China, India, Mauitius, Madiera, Siam, Arabia, and Europe. Elias was brazen enough to become a rival with the East India, the Holland, the French, and Swedish chartered companies. His most prized ship was the Grand Turk which was mounted with 22 guns that took many prizes during the Revolutionary War. The Grand Turk was later sent to various Orient ports. Jonathan Ingersoll who owned the House of Seven Gables was one of his captains to sail her. Other captains who sailed various ships for him were Thomas Perkins, Jonathan Hodges, Ebenezer West, Benjamin Hodges, John Felt, William Webb, Benjamin Crowninshield, Joseph Smith, Nathaniel Silsbee, John Prince, Daniel Bray Jr, Thomas West, and Isaac Kilham.

The Derby's shared ownership of many ships with other prominent members of Salem like Benjamin Pickman, Nathaniel West, Samuel Barton, Daniel Brookhouse, Joseph Ropes, Abel Lawrence, and Joseph Cabot.

Elias Hasket Derby Jr. returned on the Mount Vernon in 1799 to Salem after somewhat becoming a hippie of the day visiting India and the Red Sea. He had been running the family business from overseas from India. He marries Lucy Brown in 1797. He continued in service for his father till he receives a letter stating his death in 1799. At that time Elias Jr. inherited the new mansion his father built on property confiscated from the Brown family as they fled to Canada during the Revolutionary War. The mansion was a money pit and his ventures as a merchant was failing. After a semi-retirement of 10 years he was forced again to find a trade. He tried going back to shipping. He bought the Mount Hope and sailed to Rio Janeiro to buy sugar to sell to Russia but was ill advised instead to take coffee to London where he suffered a loss. The sugar would of doubled the fortune he made on two separate trips with the Mount Vernon which were the largest profits that his father had ever made. Then from London to Lisbon he found a flock of merino sheep evading the French Army in which he saved and shipped to Salem. Spain had ban the export of merino sheep and this flock of 1,100 was to be the savior of American skins from itchy wool which American sheep produced. Two thirds of the sheep survived the tempestuous journey. They were kept at his farm called "Ten Hills" in the Boston area to eventually spread throughout the country. Elias Hasket Derby Jr. was the first person in Massachusetts to operate a broad cloth loom in 1812. The sheep saved what was left of his fortune.

In 1815 he sold Derby Square that encompassed the mansion to John Derby III and Benjamin Pickman Jr. The mansion and gardens had been closed for years.

Was his 10 year retirement aligned with the beginning of the digging of the tunnels in town. Was he truly idle for 10 years? In 1801 Elias Hasket Derby Jr. took over the Second Corp of Cadets. Then Derby raised $2,500 to put the Commons in better condition for a training field. Now the common was quite marshy, uneven, had a few hills, and several small ponds. Derby had the hills taken down and filled in the swamps and ponds. He made the neighborhood more appealing and enticed several of his friends to build two brick houses next to each other to build the tunnels through at a fixed distance apart from each other. A route that led from ship to secret warehouses to terminate into various stores and banks downtown. Some even entered the back of the bank vaults. They used this dirt from digging tunnels to fill in the Commons, Collins Cove, and the South River on the sly. With Jefferson enforcing the Customs agents with new power with military backing to support the country, Elias Jr. (Gen. Derby) found many willing members of higher society to take part in his smuggling plan. Also he had a drawbridge placed across the South River where New Derby and Central Street is now which impeded the traffic to his competition's wharfs. By 1805 his plan was in full swing.

In 1815 Elias Hasket Derby Jr. retired to Londonberry, N.H. and became a great patron of the city. Beforehand he enjoyed gardening at his farm in Danvers. In 1826 he died in Londonberry a few months after his wife Lucy. He left behind 4 sons and 3 daughters. His son Elias Hasket Derby III learned law from his father's friend Daniel

Webster, became engaged in the business of building iron clads, and dealing in railroad law. He becomes president of Old Colony Railroad. Ezekiel Hersey Derby took over the family farms in South Fields in Salem, and built the Maynes Block on Essex directly opposite Derby Square (Derby Square Bookstore and the site of Roger Conant's house). His summer home was the Lafayette House in South Salem on the corner of Ocean an Lafayette Streets. Richard Derby moves to Newport R.I. Their sister Elizabeth marries Captain Nathaniel West. Antiss Derby marries Hon. Benjamin Pickman (Massachusetts Representative and Senator. Later a Federalist Representative in the U.S. Congress) and Patty Derby marries Hon. John Prince.

After Elias Jr. left Salem the torch passed to John Derby III and Benjamin Pickham Jr. They turned Derby Square into a honey comb of tunnels. John Derby III was also one of the merchant's along with Judge Story, Nathaniel Silsbee, Robert Stone, Stephen White, and Joseph Peabody who selected the old Crowninshield property to be the home of the new Customs House in 1819.

I have not been inside the Derby House basement as of yet because I keep missing my appointment with my friend who is a park ranger...

Basement doors are not historical and were placed onto the houses at later times. Usually utilizing the tunnel entrances to the house

In this picture you can see the erosion that has happened over the years. At one time this arch to the left would of been under ground. Below is a picture just within the shadow of the arch, you can see the addition.

5. Derby Street Taverns

At one point Derby Street and the streets connecting to it
was home to many Irish in Salem. They enjoyed patronizing
Irish bars. Later the Polish moved in and their merchants
opened their own bars leaving the Irish to exclaim they
would never drink in a Polish bar. Alas one Polish man was
smarter than the Irish barkeeps and charged a nickel to the
Irish dime per beer. Now being true Irishmen, they could
not turn down a good deal and drank from then on in at the
Polish bar. This bar was on the site of Tammany Hall and
is now the current offices of Tache Realty. Other taverns
and brothels dotted the street servicing the sailors and their
captains. Captains had discreet tunnels into the brothels to
meet up with the ladies and a good escape route during a
raid. Also these tunnels provided means to shanghai sailors.
As late as the 1950's this was an area fathers would worn

their daughters to avoid so they would not be mistaken for the ladies of the night. My friend who told me this tale mentioned she knew an old man when she was little in the 50's who had almost drowned in the tunnels as a boy he got lost as the water was coming in from Derby Wharf.

6. House of the Seven Gables
115 Derby Street

The House of the Seven Gables was built by a sea captain and merchant named John Turner in 1668. Three generations of the Turner family lived here before being sold to Captain Samuel Ingersoll in 1782. Ingersoll died at sea leaving the property to his daughter Susanna, a cousin of famed author Nathaniel Hawthorne. Hawthorne's visits here inspired the setting and title of his 1851 novel The House of the Seven Gables.

An interesting story from 1765 tells of Hawthorne's ancestor John Hathorne inheriting a tract of land from an Indian chief named Robin Hood in 1666 that began a long standing property dispute which is featured in "The house of the Seven Gables". I wondered if these smugglers ever acted like Robin Hood?

In 1692 John Turner Jr. inherited the house and added the secret stairs that led behind the rebuilt fireplace he added. The Philip's House on Essex Street also had a secret door to hide people because of the Witch Trials. It was said that after the runaway slaves entered through the tunnels they had to crawl through they would sneak up the secret staircase to a hidden room. My friend who was a telephone repairman had seen the tunnel when he was doing some work in the basement.

Secret Stairs to the second floor that runs next to the chimney in the center of the house.

7. Matthew Barton House
11 Turner Street

Matthew Barton built this home in 1683. Mariner Richard
Simons had constructed the cellar and frame before his
death. Barton had finished its construction. The house
was still standing in 1702. In 1778 Edward A. Holyoke
forecloses on the property he mortgaged to John Marsh
and has him thrown into jail. Then in 1794 Holyoke sells
the lot to mariner Benjamin McDonald and his wife Marry
(Southern Essex County Registry of Deeds Bk. 157 Pg.
193). In 1803 Mary McDonald dies. Captain John Mack
bordered this property to the north prior to 1809. Captain
John Mack was a member of the Salem Light Infantry 1888.
He sailed the Galen for Jonathan Gardner and John Fairfield
in 1798.

The house has two chimneys on the west side that are on the exterior walls of the house. One chimney is painted white. White chimneys with a black stripe were signs of support for England during the Revolutionary War. The second chimney from the left corner has a false floor in its arch. The arch has a door on it similar to the one in the Francis Boardman House. Upside down glass bottles buried in the dirt still can be seen of the original basement floor. In the back right of the basement is a narrow hall that leads to a tunnel entrance. This hall is filled with soot. The same soot can be seen in an arch in the Carousel House off the Commons on pleasant Street across from the old Washington Square Inn. Soot can also be found in the tunnel in front of the Downing Block.

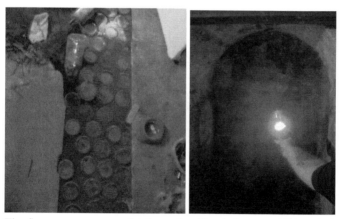

The floor once was completely made of bottle bottoms. This strip is all that remains. Inside this arch there was a hollow floor that concealed the entrance to the tunnel system. This arch also had a door still attache d to it.

8. Philips Wharf
Blaney Street

When they were dredging the harbor and making improvements in the parking lot for the new cruise ships that will disembark here I seen many utility lines merging here with some of the manhole being 12 feet deep. Most likely there were several tunnels leading here which have been converted over to carry utility lines.

In a funny story I just barely lifted my cell phone from my its case on my belt when the phone flew 25 feet into the open manhole. This area to the right as you look toward the ocean used to have a haunted house. Plus when you try to photograph Mackey's sculptures to the left made out of scarp iron you will find the strangest warning messages on your phone, the batteries will drain, and orbs will be seen on the final picture. This area does not like cameras for my cell phone had is now floating in the harbor. This was the site of Philip's Wharf.

Mackey who created all of these sculptures has been walking through a lot of the tunnels in town for years while he was fixing the utilities that run under the city. He probably has many of them on film as my friend Woody goes into the holes with video cameras to ascertain their condition for his clients. One day I will be able to meet him and ask him more.

Recently they dug up Blaney Street. 6 separate utility lines converged on this point. Some of the open manholes were 12 feet deep. When they tore up the old bulkhead on the water they found some architectural scrolling embellishments cast in plaster used as fill. a open manhole.

9. Daniel's House
1 Daniel's Street

Stephen Daniel's a shipwright built this house in 1667. In
1756 his great-grandson Samuel Silsbee, carpenter, added on
to the house. In the 1800's the house was divided between
the Russells, Hodges, and Reeds. The tunnel is in the back
left corner and the front right corner. The back right corner
you can see a change in the brick and a modern door is put
in leading to the side of the house on Essex Street. In front
of the portal leading out of the basement is a hole in the
floor with the characteristic sewer pipe leading up through
it. The tunnel entrance on the right is now a stone staircase
leading into the other side of the house.

The tunnel entrance has long since been replaced by this basement door. As you remember from before basement doors were not historically added to this basements. They are after thoughts utilizing a no longer used tunnel entrance. To the left you can see the irregular pattern of the cinder blocks as they meet the original bricks..

10. Sage-Webb-Wilkins House
52 Essex Street

This house was built in 1800 by a Scotsman named Daniel
Sage who married into the Silsbee family. He married
Stephen Daniel's' great-grand daughter. He was the captain
of the "Elizabeth" which was owned by William Gray. He
also was a Mason in 1831. There are two fireplace arches
to the right of he house on the northeast side and 3 fireplace
arches on the left side. On the roof there is only 4 chimneys..
You can see the holes in the center of the arches that would
draw air through the tunnels. The arch to the front left has a
stoop built into it similar to the one which is in the White-
Lord house. This house was connected to the tunnels and the
Daniel's House.

In this picture you can see the arch in the basement and the raised cold sill. In the picture to the left you can see the draw hole in the roof of the arch. Because of the grade outside the entrance would of had to come up through the floor.

11. Hodges House
81 Essex Street at Orange Street

Built in 1788 for the merchant John Hodges to give to his son Benjamin. In its history the Meek, Webb, and Hodges family owned it. This is the most infamous house that is attached to the tunnel system. The curator of the Witch House had seen them expose the tunnel in the backyard. Jim McAlister, Salem's noted historian from N.J., almost walked into them but was dissuaded by the water and the rats in them. I have seen the stairway that used to lead down into the tunnel or a subbasement which was concrete shut in a weird DNA spiral. I have seen the fireplace arches, but I did not get to see the section of the house which had the trapdoor in the kitchen.

John Hodges built the house to give to his son Benjamin

who was the first president of the Salem East India Marine
Society. His son Jonathan Hodges was their secretary and
Jacob Crowninshield was the treasurer. Their main purpose
was to assist the widows and children of their members,
improve navigation, and to collect oddities from areas
beyond the Cape of Good Hope and Cape Horn. It was
founded Oct. 14 1799 and had 348 members. All members
had to have been captains or supercargoes who have
rounded the Cape of Good Hope or Cape Horn.

Their museum was opened in Nov. of that year in the
Stearns Buiding on the northeast corner of Washington and
Essex Streets (Fountain Place Dinner). Then it moved to
the Old Bank Building where the present Downing Block
is (Gene Murray Dance Studio and Witch Tees) in 1804.
Following that it moved into the current home of the
Philips Library and the building that still reads the Essex
Institute next to the old armory. From 1804 to 1820 the
museum resided here. Also to share these buildings were
the Salem Athenaeum, the Historical and Natural History
Societies, and the Essex Institute. The Marine Hall on Essex
Street next to the oriental garden was built in 1824 to house
the museum in its final location. The Peabody Academy
of Sciences (161 Essex Street) was formed in 1868 from a
grant of George Peabody who was living in London at the
time. On a side note, George Peabody floated J.P. Morgan
enough money while in England to bribe the English not to
outfit the Confederates with a Navy till payment could be
had from Washington. The Peabody Academy of Science
merged the Natural History of the Essex Institute, and the
Salem East India Society museum because he found their
museums wanting and retains the name of the Peabody
Academy of Science. He buys the Marine Hall and refits
them to exhibit the two museums in. The Ethnological

Museum of the Essex Institute remains separate until 1992 when it was merged with the Peabody Academy of Science to become the Peabody Essex Museum.

In 1766 the Salem Marine Society was formed to improve the knowledge of our coast to make navigation more safe. Their headquarters was in the Franklin Building which was on the site of the present Hawthorne Hotel. Their headquarters to this day still rest on top of the new building. Their records were saved by the Essex Institute and now are owned by the Peabody Essex Museum. They are still active, but I doubt they are still concerned with the mapping of our coast since this has been accomplished some years prior.

So I ask you, with tunnels leading from the sea into the Stearns Building, the Downing Block, and the current Peabody Essex Museum, what is the real bulk of the Peabody Essex Museum entail? What wonders of art, opulence, and religious antiquities could be in their basements and attics throughout Salem? With endowments coming in from various ship captains who have been dead for over 200 years filling their coffers annually of a million dollars or more a piece, where do they apply those funds? What else besides the Russian Crown Jewels, have they scurried away into their collection?

Elias Hasket Derby was a cousin of the Hodges and a member of the Salem Marine Society. The two groups were indirectly joined by them. Elias Hasket Derby Jr. houses the Second Corp of Cadets in the Franklin Building right next to the Salem Marine Society. Also to this day the Hawthorne Hotel has expanded on their exclusive rights to offer bar service at all of the museums functions to being the only caterer aloud from time to time. The two buildings are still closely linked by commerce and tunnels.

12. The Bunghole
204 Derby Street

Opened in 1933. This building used to be a funeral home
during prohibition. At that time the owner and his friends
would meet in the basement to drink illegally. They would
lean over and whisper to each other "I will meet you in the
Bunghole." One of the friends suggested if prohibition
would be lifted that they should turn the building into a
liquor store. So he did in 1933 and his relative who was
about to be ordained as a Polish priest suggested "The
Bunghole" for the name. They had the 2nd liquor license to
be issued in the city after prohibition. So the corpses moved
out, the embalming tubes buried in the walls, and the tunnels
were closed. Every morning a line of poor souls wait at the

door who look like the embalmed clients of this buildings past.

Now many distilleries like Col. Lawrence's on Front Street had tunnels running from them. Since smuggling molasses was a time honored profession in Salem. Just during prohibition, the molasses went in above ground and the liquor went under. The tunnels would be the safest way for this social drinkers to get embalmed. So if you are thirsty, make sure you get yours in "The Bunghole".

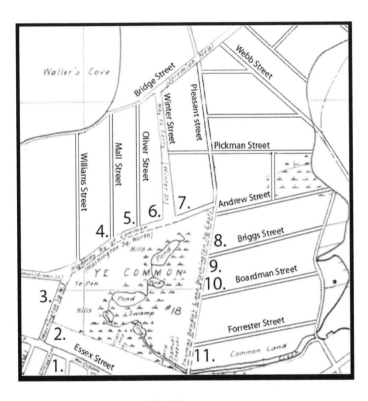

The Commons

Chapter 2

Commons

The Commons had a creek that ran into the ocean.
It started where the basketball court is and ran
parallel to Washington Square East and turned and
ran down what is now Forrester Street towards the
Ocean. Land on the north side of Forrester was also
land held in common to the town. The creek had five
ponds in total attached to it. There was Flag pond
that formed after heavy rains to the southeast; then
opposite Southwick's School House was Southwick
Pond; opposite Captain Mason's was Mason's Pond;
then to the east of that was Cheever's Pond across
from Cheever's tannery; and one near the school
house by Forrester Street was Lang's Pond. Also it
had included several hills and hillocks. This area was
used to graze unfenced livestock, gather berries, cut
flags and hoops. Ducks, horses, cattle, geese, hens,
and stray pigs ran free in the Commons. It had several
names including "pen", "Town Swamp", "Training Field",
"Washington Square", and "Salem Common".

Previous to 1714 there were disputes between
cottagers and commoners who had rights to the
swamp. The Rev. John Higgison had a house on
the north of the Commons and Col. John Higgison
had a house where the Hawthorne Hotel is now.
In 1714 the Commons was voted to be forever a
training field for the use of Salem's militia in front of
Higginson's house.

In 1772 an almshouse was built on the northeast
corner on Washington Square South. Also there were

a powder house, engine house, and a tavern owned by
Beadle. This street was home to the Philips School
House and the Southwick School House.

On Washington Square East there was the Captain
Francis Boardman house built in 1782. The land was
owned by John Hodges. Next was the house of Joseph
Vincent with his rope walk in the rear running to the
Cove and next north of that a two story house owned
and occupied by Thomas Briggs. Then an old building
which had been occupied by Benjamin Brown as a
bake house. Briggs street was not then opened. It was
first a Court extending about two thirds the length
of the street. Briggs's Rope Walk commenced at the
place now occupied by Hon. Nathaniel Silsbee's house
(Knights of Columbus) and extended to the Cove.
Andrew street was not opened till after the Common
was leveled. The field extending from north of Briggs's
Rope Walk (to the north of the house which was owned
by William B. Vincent which was built in 1799) was
owned by Col. William Browne who bought it from
Capt. Joseph Gardner who was slain in the battle with
the Narragansetts in 1675. Col. William Browne will
have all of his property in Salem confiscated after
fleeing to Canada during the Revolutionary War,
including what would become Derby Square. Vincent's
grandson Jonathan A. Vincent carried on the tanning
and currying business there until it was sold in 1791
to another William Browne and his son who continued
the tannery until they opened Andrew Street and
sold it off as house lots. The Full-Spychalski Funeral
Home stands where Dr. Hardy Phippen house was
and earlier to that it was Benjamin Ives tan yard and
bark house. This site was also a ropewalk owned by
Joseph Vincent which stretch to Collins Cove as well.

In 1785 a school was built on the commons. In

1788 the Beverly Bridge was opened and Pleasant Street was extended from the commons to meet Bridge Street. Also after the opening of the bridge Winter Street and Bath Street (Forrester Street) was created. Hay scales were erected on Winter Street in 1789 in front of a pond next to Robert Upton's house half way up the road.

On Washington Square North was the Samuel Cheever house who had a tannery in the rear. Then there was James Wright bakery. On the corner of Oliver was Mr. Austin's's brass founder shop. After that was Jeremiah Shepard's grocery store, behind that runs an alley to Rev. John Higginson's mansion. Next was Jonathan Mason's shop (the mason William Roberts lived in this home after it was moved to Federal Street) followed by Fredrick Coom's Bakery, The Collins house, Tutle's Rope Walk, Henry Williams on Williams Street, Thadeus Gwinn ropewalk, Nehemiah Adams cabinet maker, and the East Church (Witch Museum).

On Hawthorne Blvd. was a school house and the Gardner-Pingree Mansion.

Other facts of the Commons. In 1769 Thomas Row and Robert Wood were tarred and feather on a Liberty Tree for informing on the Salem privateers to the Crown.

Then in 1801 Elias Hasket Derby Jr. commanded the Second Corp. of Cadets to fill in the ponds and grade the Commons. The Commons was leveled by the Spring of 1802. Derby had raised a subscription of $2,500 to do so and planted rows of poplars and surrounded it with a whitewashed oak fence. The poplars came from the nursery owned by Joseph Franks on what is now Winter Street.

The bills was:

ESTIMATE OF THE COMMITTEE

15000 feet of lumber for railing and posts at $10 per hundred is
$156.00

Labor on the above one man 60 days at 9s
$90.00

Ditto one man for digging post holes Ac 60 days at 6s
60.00

Poplar trees 10 feet apart at Is apiece
100.00

Expenses for Drink
20.00

1 lb of paint will paint 3 square yard twice over 3s 1733 square
feet
577 lb White Lead is equal to 5 ewt at $13 per ewt
65.00

10 Galls boiled Oil at 8s per GaM
14.00

20 days work for painting at 6s par day
20.00

For Leveling say
1,000.00

For Gravel Walk say
1,000.00

Stone Gutter
100.00

Total:$26,25.00

They received a loan from Benjamin A. Gray that
159 subscribers to the Commons improvement*

paid back. Some gave twice when funds fell short.
The biggest contributors were William Gray, Elias
Hasket Derby Jr., George Crowninshield & Sons
Co., and Joseph Peabody. Now out of this list we
have two subscribers who were block and pump
makers, two who owned hardware stores, two
were auctioneers to fence the goods, a carpenter
who opens up a coffee shop in Boston afterwards,
several people working for the Customs Agency
(Bartholomew Putnam Surveyor of Port, Henry
Tibbets Inspector of Customs, C. Cleavland Deputy
Collector, Elijah Haskell Inspector of Customs,
James Cheever Officer in the Customs House,
Benjamin Crowninshield Collector of Marblehead,
Penn Townsend Revenue Agent, Henry Prince's son
captained a Revenue Cutter, Joseph Hiller Customs
Collector), 3 presidents of insurance companies, 4
store owners, 5 distillers smuggling molasses again, 4
tavern keeps, 4 politicians, 2 judges, 3 dry good store
owners, 2 hardware store owners, 2 ropewalk owners,
4 grocers, 4 in local government, 2 butchers, 2 die at
sea, 1 murdered, 2 Clerks of Courts, several Masons,
several merchants and captains, several relatives of
Hodges, Derby, Peabody, and Crowninshield. So you
have a group of captains and merchants who need
to smuggle goods pass a series of bribed Customs
employees and politicians. Then convince a group of
merchants to construct new homes to attach to the
tunnels on the Commons to move money and goods
through. These tunnels will need to be pumped out of
water so carpenters, muscle provided by the several
militias, and masons could create them utilizing
hardware and rope from other subscribers. These
tunnels will smuggle goods into several stores to sell
dry goods and food, molasses to the distillers to make
spirits, flour and spices to the bakers, liquor for the
taverns to sell, auctioneers to sell your big ticket items,

and banks to hide your money away tax free.

In 1802 the selectmen changed its name to Washington Square. 1803 a bath house was placed on Bath Street (Forrester Street). In 1817 the popular trees gave place to Elms and a new wooden fence was put in. In 1850 the iron fence was installed at the cost of $7,000 by Messrs. Denio, Cheney and Co. of Boston. After these improvements in 1801 Derby started getting his accomplices to build 2 brick Federal Style mansions set apart from each other the distance between the Derby House on Essex Street and the Hodges House on Orange Street. The industrial and agricultural appearance of the Commons became opulent. These house were to be used to run the tunnels through town to the jail, courts, each others homes, banks, and the businesses downtown. There is even rumors that the tunnels lead under the Commons. There is a square iron cover over a cement shaft in front of the Knights of Columbus and a round manhole cover in front of the 1926 Gazebo. Who knows...

Tunnel entrance in front of Knights of Columbus in the Commons.

1. Brown Building 2-4 Union Street and 105-107 Essex Street

The Brown Building was built in 1808-1809 on property once owned by the Brown family. It has been called the Union Building, Merchant's, and the Brown Building. The Merchant's Bank, William Stearns Apothecary, and several professional and religious offices, educational facilities, and retail stores have been in here. John Watson (William B. Parker's father-in-law) had a school house here. Manning's Stage stables was next door on Union Street. Manning was Hawthorne's uncle. The Merchant's Bank was organized in 1811 and later moved to the Bowker Block (Sun Tavern and the modern offices of the Peabody Essex Museum) and then the Asiatic Building. Its presidents were Benjamin Crowninshield, Jospeh Story, John W. Treadwell, Benjamin H. Silsbee. It became a national bank in 1865.

Towards the alley behind the dry cleaners there is an exterior chimney pointing towards Archer's house. Another three line up parallel to Essex Street where the tunnel runs.

2. Hawthorne Hotel
18 Washington Square West at Essex Street

Possible the first Catholic mass was said in a small house

on this lot before the Franklin Building by Abbe de la Poterie. Col. John Higginson, son of Rev. Higginson, house was built on this spot in 1675 and was torn down in 1809. In 1714 they desired the training field should forever be in front of his house. Nathaniel Andrew marries into the Higginson family and the property comes into the possession of the Andrew family. In 1762 Nathaniel leaves the property in his will to his youngest son John Andrew. This corner will be known as Andrew Corner. John Andrew sells the property to John Gardner before moving to Windham, Maine. In 1809 John Gardner sells the property to Samuel Archer 3rd who tears down the house to build the Archer Block. Samuel Archer 3rd was part of the firm Andrew & Archer with John Andrew (The grandson of John Andrew who sold the property to John Gardner).

The Archer Block was finished in 1810 by Samuel McIntire to house residential apartments, offices, and retail stores on Andrew's Corner. By 1810 Samuel Archer 3rd dies and his estate sells the Archer Block to Josiah Dow who was a dry goods dealer and he named the building Wakefield Place after the town he was born in Vermont.. Then in 1811 he sold it to Thomas Perkins.

Thomas Perkins and Joseph Peabody were officers on the brig Ranger in 1782 on the Potomac River and repulsed 3 British Tory barges killing 50 British sailors. Later the two would become privateers and become partners in commercial business. From 1789 to 1801 they were co-owners of the Cynthia, Nabby, Neptune, Cincinnati, Sally, and Tabitha. Later in life Perkins partnered with Michael Shepard. The two of them were members of the Salem Marine Society. Thomas Perkins and his brother James was successful trading opium from India for tea in China.

Thomas was the supercargo for Derby when he sent the
first ship to Canton from U.S. He was president of the
Boston branch of the National Bank and was elected as
a Federalist 8 times to the U.S. Senate. With his profits
he invested them in mills, Perkins Institute for the Blind,
Mass General Hospital, the Boston and Lowell Railroad, the
Boston and Providence Railroad, and many other railroads
out west. John Cushing was raised by his uncle Thomas
on his mother Ann's death. He would become in charge of
the Hong, trading house, in China for his uncle. Cushing
dealt with Houqua, the head of the Cohong, who was the
most powerful in China at the time. Also Caleb Cushing
was elected to the House of Representatives in 1843 after
President Harrison's suspicious death. President Tyler sent
him to China as U.S. Commissioner. He secured 5 ports
in China and continued the family business more than
Tyler's. John Murray Forbes started in his uncles James'
and Thomas' counting house and was later sent to replace
Cushing in Canton to run the opium business and stayed
till 1837. He left for Canton in the year of the death of
Thomas and presided in the opium boom from 1821-1837.
Then Russell Sturgis marries Thomas' sister Elizabeth.
Russell's son James Perkins Sturgis was sent to the island
of Lintin to manage the storage facilities that housed the
Opium. Sturgis teamed with George Robert Russell in
the firm Russell and Company. Barings Bank headed by
Russell Sturgis financed Russell and Company. Sturgis
daughter Elizabeth Perkins Sturgiss marries John Pierpont
Morgan 2nd. Samuel Russell continued the work in Canton
having Warren Delano Jr. as his rival, Franklin Delano
Roosevelt's grandfather. Then for you conspiracy thinkers,
Samuel Russell's cousin William Huntington Russell was
the cofounder of the Skull and Bones with Alfonso Taft....
Thomas Perkins dies in 1830, 9 years before the opium trade

becomes illegal prompting the Opium War with Britain. Although not illegal at the time, Perkins' trade in slaves and opium was indeed immoral.

In 1818 the building was renamed the Franklin Building. It caught on fire in 1845, 1859, and was razed in 1860 when the insurance just expired only a few hours earlier. In 1864 a new Franklin Building was built. In 1924 the Hawthorne Hotel was built and the Statue of Nathaniel Hawthorne was moved from its home in the Museum of Fine Arts to the park next to the hotel.

The Franklin Building has housed the Salem Marine Society, a home for aged sailors, the armories of Salem Independent Cadets, Salem Second Corp of Cadets, Salem Light Infantry, Co. K, 8th Mass. Regt. on the third floor, Charles Parker's first toy store, Saltonstall High School for Girls, and the post office in 1816 when Joseph E. Sprague succeeded John Dabney. Subscribers to the Common Improvement Amos Harvey and John Scobie also had dry goods store on the first floor. The militias had two large halls and anterooms. In 1835 the Essex County Natural History Society in its second year was stored on the 4th floor of the building till 1837.

The Salem Marine Society was instituted in 1766 and incorporated in 1772. It was composed of captains and owners of vessels who helped improve the navigation of our coasts and relieve the poor of its members and families in need of assistance. Thomas Perkins who made his fortune in the opium trade and slaves and founded the Perkins Institute for the Blind bequeathed the Franklin Building that was worth $15,000 in 1833 to the Society. Upon their death many other members remembered the society in their wills to aid the widows and destitute sailors who abstained from drink. Captain Nathaniel West donated Derby Wharf to them. The will was contested for a time and they profited $12,500. They had numerous shares in the Salem National Bank, Salem National Exchange Bank, Merchant's National Bank, and the Asiatic Bank. Several of these banks had tunnels running through them.

In 1996 I had seen the road fall in between the Hawthorne Hotel and the Brown Building. The hole extended both sides of the road for 5 car lengths. Most likely this was from the tunnel caving in. There are two rectangular open faced manhole lids covering shafts that could of once have entered the buildings around where the sales offices are in the basement and the employee mens room. These openings can be seen all of the way down Essex Street to North Street. They were dog legs so one group pushing a cart of cargo can back up and scoot to one side to allow another to pass.

The fact that Elias Hasket Derby Jr. headquartered the Second Corp of Cadets here and was a member of the Salem Marine Society at the time of his digging the tunnels, all fingers point to this being connected. Also two subscribers of the Commons Improvement had shops here that could of received goods to sell through the tunnels duties free...

3. Andrew-Safford House
13 Washington Square West at Brown Street

Built in 1818 by David Lord for John Andrew who was part of Andrew & Archer. Andrew & Archer built the Franklin Building where the Hawthorne Hotel now stands. Him and his partner were subscribers to the Common Improvement Fund. John had made his fortune selling furs from Russia and probably had made deals with the tanneries on Winter Street who were also subscribers.

Now the 2 exterior chimneys run parallel to the road leading to the tunnels intersection at Essex Street. Another exterior chimney points towards the armory, but seems inconclusive . For sometime it was the house of the director of the Peabody Essex Museum, but seems to have been unused for years. I have not at this point gained access to this home, so I can only say speculatively that it was connected by its location in between the Forrester-Peabody House and the tunnels running on Essex Street and Andrew's connection to the Franklin Building.

4. Forrester-Peabody House
29 Washington Square at Mall Street

Built in 1819 on the site of the Mason House which was
moved to Federal Street where mason William Roberts
resided. The house was built in 1768 for Jonathan Mason.
William Roberts had built the house down the road on the
corner of Winter Street, the East India Marine Hall, the
Bowker Block, and St. Peter's Church. John Fairfield
subscriber to the Commons Improvement lived here till
1814 when he moved to Londonberry N.H. to herd sheep for
Elias Hasket Derby Jr. . John Forrester the son of merchant
Simon Forrester lived here till Col. George Peabody bought
it in 1834. Peabody lived here to 1892 entertaining the likes
of Longfellow, Lowell, and Agassiz. The Salem Club was
in here. Now it is the Bertram Home for Men. The Bertram
Home for Men serves as an assisted living home.

The tunnels run under the addition the one floor addition that houses the dinning room and makes a right turn to the rear to connect to the basement of the Carriage House. From the carriage house the tunnel leads out the back toward Bridge Street. It is blocked off by a modern stairs and Bilco door. On the opposite corner there was three tunnels running next to each other. Two are blocked off with the third remaining to be later blocked off by a stairs and Bilco door as well.

The first photo show the right tunnel leading to the back. Then you turn left and walk behind the other two tunnels and exit to the right through a stairs out of the basement to the backyard on the left of the house.

Portrait of Longfellow.

5. White-Lord House
31 Washington Square North at Oliver Street

Stephen White had Joshua Upham build this house in
1811 on the site of the old James Wright Bakery, Mr.
Austin's brass founder shop, and Jeremiah Shepard's
grocery store. There also was an alley running to Rev.
Higginson's mansion. Joshua Upham (1784-1858) would
build the Pickman-Derby Block as well in which I have
been in the old wine cellar that was converted out of a
stretch of the tunnels. He also was one of a committee
amongst John Derby III, Nathaniel Silsbee, Robert Stone,
and Joseph Peabody who chose to place the Customs House
in 1819 on the site of the old George Crowninshield home.
Joshua Upham would build Old Town Hall, Pickman-
Derby block (Behind Derby Square Bookstore) in 1817,
Pickman Building (22-26 Front Street and 15 Derby

Street which houses Maria Sweet Something), White-Silsbee/Hodges-Mott House, Judge Story House, and the Lawrence Block. All attached by tunnels.

Stephen White was the nephew of Captain Joseph White who was murdered in 1830. The Committee of Vigilance was created among 27 men with the power to search every house and interrogate every individual touching the murder. The group met at Stephen White's house nightly on the Commons and was given $1,000 and sworn to secrecy. Strangely enough Stephen hired no detectives nor informed the Sheriff. When Judge Story heard about the murder he grabbed Stephen by the collar and shook him violently accusing him. A letter was sent by a Grant stating that he and Stephen hit Captain White with a large piece of led and stabbed him with a dirk. The coroner report shows that the blow to the head killed him and there was two separate knives of different lengths had stabbed him 13 times. The knife wounds produced no blood...

In 1826 he had owned the Caroline and Joseph J. Knapp Jr. was its captain. After the death of his wife and mother he takes the brunt of it out on Joseph J. Knapp Jr. and never gives him a ship again. In wake of this Knapp marries his cousin which irritates him even more. The Knapp brothers would in the end hang for Captain White's murder.

Stephen inherits $250,000 from his uncle on his death. Six of Judge Story's nieces receive $25,000 a piece. Captain Joseph White's will was changed right before his death. Stephen White also hires Samuel Lorenzo Knapp of the Boston Gazette to publish a biography of Daniel Webster who prosecuted the Knapp brothers.

Stephen White was the son of Captain Henry White (dead in 1824) who was Captain Joseph White's brother. Stephen's brother was Joseph "Junior" White out of respect to his uncle. They lived next to each other in mansions on the Commons connected to their uncle's home by means of tunnels. They had a third brother named Francis White. Stephen's and Joseph junior's homes were connected to Stephen's brother-in-law's house, Judge Joseph Story. Joseph "Junior" White had died in 1819 and his wife Eliza or Betsy, Judge Story's sister, lived in the home up to 1831 when she sold it to the Silsbee family.

In 1832 Stephen was chairman of the Massachusetts Convention of National Republicans that turned into the Whig Party. Stephen was nominating Daniel Webster to be their candidate. The party nominated Henry Clay instead to go against President Andrew Jackson and lost. Stephen was hoping to be the man behind Daniel Webster in the White House. Webster hung back though hoping to be aligned with Jackson but failed.

Stephen dies in 1835 in New York City. He had left three daughters. Stephen was married to Harriet Story who also gave him 3 daughters, the White Witches. They were the belles of the invitation only balls of Boston. One of them married Daniel Webster's son Col. Daniel Fletcher Webster and the other married Daniel Webster's brother-in-law J. William Paige. Before his death Stephen was elected several times to both branches of legislature, made a fortune in Turkish opium and seal skins, and incorporated the East India Marine Hall Company to cover the liability that might arise from the new East India Marine Hall with his Asiatic Bank and Oriental Insurance Office on the ground floor. Stephen was also the first president of the Asiatic Bank and president of the Salem East India Marine Society in 1823. His wharf was 3rd to the right from Derby Wharf on Becket Street. He also headed the Society for the Detection of Thieves and Robbers.

I have been in the basement of this building and have seen the tunnels in the old fireplace arches blocked off. It has a brick basement floor allowing for smooth transport of cargo on carts through the tunnels into this basement. The back right chimney did have a cooking fireplace in it that might have been left behind by the old baker.

6. White-Silsbee/Hodges-Mott House: 33-35 Washington Square North at Oliver Street

The White-Silsbee House was built in 1812. This is the oldest section of this adjoined house that resides at 33

Washington Square North (Used to be 2 Oliver Street).
Joshua Upham had built this house. Joseph "Junior" White
was Stephen's brother and Captain Joseph White's nephew.
Joseph married Joseph Story's sister Betsy in 1808. He
had three daughters Elizabeth who married Samuel C.
Gray, Mary Barrow White who married George W. Pratt,
and Charlotte Sophia. He had owned several ships along
with George Crowninshield, William Manning, his brother
Stephen White, Joseph J. Knapp, William Parker, Nathaniel
Silsbee, Robert Stone, Henry Prince, Henry White Jr.,
and John Dodge Jr. . This home had several balls with the
finest wines that Joseph could import. He was the town's
favorite. Joseph "Junior" White dies in 1819. Betsy remains
in the house till 1831 and sells it to the Silsbee family. The
Silsbees owned it till 1880.

The newer house attached to the right was built in 1841
for Hannah and Betsy Hodges. Hannah inherited outright
when Betsy died in 1851. This house was on the old Samuel
Cheever lot who had a tannery in the rear. John Mott buys it
in 1871. In 1924 it was bought by the Clarks who owned it
and the White-Silsbee House attached to it.

This home also is connected by the tunnels through
the fireplace arches. There is also an area cut into the
floor where the sewer pies come into the basement wide
enough for a stairway at one time. The floor like the house
previously mentioned is made of brick. Also there is a
square iron plate behind a sewer drain on the corner of
Washington Square North and Winter. Someone left an old
brake shoe from a car behind that can be used to open the
cover. I stepped in and found it filled with many layers of
dead leaves. I have not as of yet come back with a shovel to
see how deep it really is.

On a side note, I am in the process of building a banquet hall in which it will be called Vingolf. It will be built on acreage once owned by Henry White who left it to Stephen in the town of Manchester-by-the-Sea.

7. Roberts-Shepard-Thorndike Double House
39-41 Washington Square at Winter Street

Mason William Roberts acquires this land in 1825 and builds this house in 1830. This was to be one of many identical homes stretching towards Pleasant Street. This was the only one to be built. In 1830 he sold the house at 39 Washington Square North to Stephen Shepard. 41 Washington Square North was sold to Larkin Thorndike in 1830 also. William Roberts was living in the old Mason House after it was moved to Federal Street.

Roberts had built the Bowker Block, Saint Peter's

Church, and The East India Marine Hall. At least two of them, the East India Marine Hall and the Bowker Block, are linked by tunnels. I have no idea if the church is at this point. It does have two exterior chimneys on the left that line up with the two houses on the right. I have not been in this home either.

8. Nathaniel Silsbee House
94 Washington Square East

Was built in 1818 on the site of Brigg's ropewalk. Nathaniel Silsbee married Marry Crowninshield in 1802. He was a shipmaster who rose to be the President of the State Senate and then a Senator in the U.S. Congress. from 1826-1835.

Daniel Webster, President Monroe, and Henry Clay had been entertained in this house by Silsbee. In 1850 his son moves out of the house to the left and into his. In 1907 the

Knights of Columbus takes over the building.

In 1844 he became the president of the Salem Savings Bank after the death of Joseph Peabody left the position vacant. Peabody held it from 1830-1844. Previous to him was Dr. Edward Holyoke. In 1818 the Salem Savings Bank opened and had Joseph White, Joseph Peabody, Benjamin Pickman Jr. , Judge Joseph Story, Jacob Ashton, and Moses Townsend as vice presidents. Trustees included Jonathan Hodges, Stephen White, and William Fettyplace. At that time it was in the Central Building where the Salem Partnership, Haunted Footsteps, and the Trolley Depot are now. In 1818 the Customs House was in the same building. It resided here from 1805-1807 and then 1813-1819. Col. William R. Lee used to own the property. In 1819 the Customs House was moved to its current site. Holyoke at his death at 100 years of age was president of the Salem Savings Bank, Essex Historical Society, Salem Dispensary, and Salem Athenaeum. In 1844 the Salem Savings Bank moved from Central Building to Pickman Place which was on the site of the current Downing Block. Pickman Place was built by Col. Pickman for the use of the Salem Marine Insurance Office, the Salem Bank, and the East India Marine Society. Above the bank was the Essex Historical Society (founded 1821). It was first in Essex Place opposite Central Street on Essex Street, then Pickman Place, and then Lawrence Place (Bleachers, Jonathan's, Roost). Benjamin Crowninshield, Nathaniel Silsbee, Benjamin Pickman, and Joseph B. Felt were members. Nathaniel Silsbee would remain president of the Salem savings Bank till his death in 1850. In 1855 the bank moved to the Asiatic Building on Washington Street (Eastern Bank).

I have not been in the basement yet, but I have noticed that the door to the basement has a modern pass key similar to the one for the Salem Marine Society on top of the Hawthorne Hotel. There is 1 exterior chimney that lines up with his sons house to the left.

9. Baldwin-Lyman House
92 Washington Square East at Briggs Street

Built in 1809 on part of the site belonging to Thomas Briggs
ropewalk and house. Samuel McIntire began construction
on the house before his death. His son Samuel Field
McIntire finished the interior. Jabez Baldwin of Baldwin
and Jones had owned it. He was a jeweler and watchmaker.
His shop was in the West's Block. He married Thomas
Briggs daughter Ana. He was a subscriber of the Commons
Improvement Fund. Jabez was one of several of Salem
leading citizens who had shares in the Palladium which was
going to run a line from Liverpool to Salem in 1816. It never
took off and the ship was sold in 1817. He dies in 1819.

This is another house I need to investigate, but it does
have 6 exterior chimneys. The one on the left lines up with

the single chimney on the Nathaniel Silsbee House and the one on the front left with the Francis Boardman House. The funeral home next door seems to be set back so not to have its foundation through the tunnel. On the site of the funeral home was Joseph Vincent's house and ropewalk who was a subscriber of the Commons Improvement Fund.

10. Francis Boardman House
82 Washington Square East at Boardman Street

This home was begun in 1782 but was not finished till 1789. It was built for Captain Francis Boardman. We have extensive logs and letters throughout his career from mate to captain which illustrate he was superstitious and believed in the "portents of dreams". He had owned many ships partnered with Nathaniel West and John Dodge which he captained himself. During the War of 1812 he owned shares in the ship Montgomery with many people including Joseph

White Jr. and Stephen White. Boardman marries Benjamin W. Crowninshield's sister Mary. The property was originally owned by George Hodges. His daughter Elizabeth marries Nathaniel Bowditch but dies early. The other daughter Mary marries Benjamin W. Crowninshield who was soon to become Secretary of the Navy. The remaining daughter Sarah marries Zachariah Fowle Silsbee and inherits the house. Their son Francis survives them all. Francis' wife Mary Boardman is a Salem Commons Improvement Fund subscriber. Captain Francis Boardman dies at 44 in 1792 at Port au Prince Hispaniola.

The house was built by the brothers Joseph and Samuel McIntire and was the first mansion on the commons. At the time of the Salem Commons Improvement Sarah and Zachariah Silsbee where living in the house. Zachariah was part of the merchant firm Stone, Silsbee & Pickman of Salem. He dies in 1783.

I have been in this basement and have seen the bricked up entrance behind a fascinating boiler that was set into the floor. The floor was dug out about a 1.5 ft. deep by 11 ft long and 4 ft wide. Before the boiler was placed in this recess it would be easy to imagine that this opening in the floor was access to a staircase going down into the tunnels. I found all of this in the back left fireplace arch. The front right arch still had a door on it. The back of the fireplace arch was bricked up though. It was being used as a closet now with a shelf running across it. The shelf was also in the Sage-Webb House across the fireplace arch.

Next door is the Captain Joseph Hosmer house built in 1795. It could possibly have an older tunnel route and entrance to it? Samuel Archer who built the Archer Building

(Hawthorne Hotel) buys the property in 1807. He added the ell running down Boardman Street at the time. The house following that was built by Captain Samuel Webb in 1770 and is the oldest home on the Commons. The famed shipbuilder Enos Brigg who built the Grand Turk lived here from 1808 to his death in 1819.

In the Boardman House their is still a door on the sealed entrance to the tunnel.

There is this large hole that a monster of a furnace sits in. Did they dig up the basement to build this furnace in place or just build it on top of the entrance to a subbasement? Similar holes can be found in the Pierce Nichols House, Old Town Hall, and the Mason Lodge.

j

Samuel Archer III lived here in 1807 when he had the Franklin building
built.

12. Clifford Crowninshield House
74 Washington Square East at Forrester Street

Was built in 1804 by Samuel McIntire at the time of
Clifford's wedding. Clifford paid twice into the Commons

Improvement Fund and was a member of the Salem East India Marine Society. He dies prematurely in 1809 at 47 and his sister obtains it and lives with her husband James Devereux in the home. Devereux was the Captain of the Franklin which was the first American vessel to trade with Japan.

I got to tour this house, but the real estate owner forgot the keys to the basement. So I need to reschedule...

63

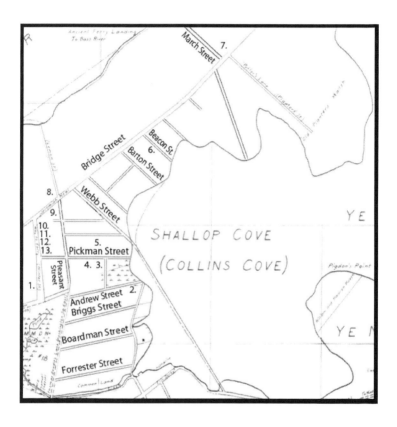

Collins Cove

-Chapter 3-

Collins Cove

Ye Sea as it was plainly called by the Old Planters who
followed Roger Conant here was the inhabitants first
home. They had houses on March Street and farms
that ran from there down to Ye Sea. Collins Cove
was their economic center where they placed their
fisheries. The Cove at one time was the heart of the
city. Prior to 1692 the Cove was dotted with fishing
cottages. In 1790 William Brown and Joseph Vincent
built a seawall where their properties meet on the
cove. They then leveled the land to the top of the wall.
A good portion of this neighborhood that runs behind
the Commons and off Bridge Street had to be filled
in to run the roads we know today. Some of these
roads like Andrews Street only opened up after the
Commons Improvement in 1801. When they ran out of
places to deposit the dirt from making the tunnels in
the Commons did they use it to fill in the areas behind
the Commons. The marshiest area being around Milk
Street off Andrew Street. They will fill in the creek
running from the Commons along Forrester Street
and its mouth in the Cove that ran from Saint Nicholas
Church to Ziggy's Donuts on Essex Street. The areas of
Collins Cove off Bridge Street will be filled in later.

Collins Cove was named Shallop Cove after all of
the Shallop ships that proliferated the cove. A shallop
is a light sailboat used mostly for coastal fishing with
one or more masts and carrying fore-and-aft or lug
sails and sometimes equipped with guns. Many left
this cove during the Revolutionary War outfitted as

Privateers. Other names for the cove included the
Sea, the Salt Sea, the Cove, Ye Sea, and the cove
near the Neck in historical writings. 1826 had seen
a committee headed by Benjamin Crowninshield
and Timothy Pickering to assess the value of placing
mills on the North River and Collins Cove to build
manufacturing plants. In March 1833 David Pingree,
Joel Bowker, Elisha Mack, Larkin Thorndike, and John
Read incorporated The Naumkeag Wharf and Whale
Fishery Company. Their wharf and warehouse used
to produce sperm candles would be around Conners
Road bordering William B. Parker's on Lathrop
Street. This was the father of the Parker Brothers
who established an empire based on board games. The
Parkers owned large tracts of land from Lathrop to
Barton Street and on March Street.

Collins Cove had extensive mud flats till they
were filled in over the years. A 1700 map shows a
bridge across the creek leading from the Commons
into Collins Cove extending from Becket Street. This
was called Virgin's Point because of three spinsters
who lived there. A path led from there to the tip of
the current Andrew Street. In 1803 the creek leading
from the Commons still existed because a bath house
had been built on its shores. By 1830 there is no
mention of the path leading from Becket Street across
the creek bridge on the map. The creek is filled in,
but there are still mud flats extending to Warren
Street. Also there are no roads from Pickman Street
to Lathrop Street on Collins Cove. Pickman, Andrew,
Briggs, and Forrester were extended to the Collins
Cove on this map. In 1869 the City Council approved
an act that was put forth in 1855 to run a road from
Essex Street to Bridge Street called Webb Street. Then
Collins Street was also approved to run from Webb
Street to Barton Street. This area will have its flats

filled in to accommodate the new streets and homes. The manholes that are marked "Sewer" run up Collins Street and half way up Barton Street. In a William B. Parker et. al. deed from 1871 mentions Beacon Street as East Watson (named after his father in-law). A 1874 map shows Collins Street connecting to East Watson Street (named after John Watson whose daughter was Abigail) with a rail leading to the Eastern Railroad Car Company (Salem Brake and Clutch). In 1884 Webb Street touched the ocean with the Essex Railroad spanning from Andrew Street to Fort Ave over a narrow strip of land with a pond in between it and Webb Street. This area is now the beach and walkway that leads from the narrow path at the end of Andrew Street and stretches past the propeller shop and into the lot across Szetela Ln. with the lobster traps. In 1884 the area bordering Szetela Ln. to north, Memorial Drive on the east, Fort Ave on the south, and Webb Street on the west were still mud flats.

So I will assume that by the time Brigadier General Elias Hasket Derby Jr. moved to Londonberry, N.H. in 1815 he had completed filling in the Commons and the creek with all the dirt from the tunnels and the hills. Filling in the rest of the mud flats on Collins Cove he left to others.

1. Joseph Story House
26 Winter Street

This house was built in 1811 for Joseph Story. His sisters married the White brothers. The year in which Elias Hasket Derby Jr. begins his plan to build a new series of tunnels in town, Joseph Story in 1801 was admitted to the bar in Salem. At the time he was the only Jeffersonian Democratic-Republican in Essex County to be admitted. He would rise to be the head of the bar in Essex County. Because of his alignment with Jefferson the firm George Crowninshield & Sons Co. had retained him. In 1805 he was elected to the Massachusetts House of Representatives alongside Stephen White. This year his wife Mary F.L. Oliver and his father would die. Joseph Story made a power move when in April 1807 Congressman Jacob

Crowninshield spat up blood while speaking in Congress
and soon died. Story was the Crowninshield family lawyer.
Benjamin Crowninshield was tapped to replace his brother
but Story took his seat in 1808 with the help of the White
brothers and his new marriage to Judge William Wetmore's
daughter Sarah Waldo Wetmore. She would give him 7
children. Story now felt that his power in Washington
and the White's power in Salem could dethrone the
Crowninshields that he had worked for.   Story lobbied for
Jefferson's downfall after the Embargo Act and became the
Federalist favorite Democratic-Republican. He only sat in
Congress for a year. Now power in Salem was truly now
in the hands of the White family and Story's. They would
start the Friday Evening Club which brought together 10
members who were friends and family to discuss affairs
of banks, insurance companies, and the local Democratic-
Republican Party. In 1811 Story became the Speaker in the
Massachusetts House of Representative.

In 1811 Joseph Story who was head of the Essex Bar
in Massachusetts was appointed to the Supreme Court at
32. He is still the youngest to ever be appointed. His main
course in the Supreme Court was to protect the property
rights of the minority of the rich men in the country. He
was a hero of Alexander Hamilton's and John Marshall's
conservative Republicanism. In his life he wrote many
books concerning his opinion on the Constitution. After
the War of 1812 Stephen White and Judge Story pushed
forward for Salem to install new sidewalk curbs, plant trees,
pave roads, and create schools. In 1819 he led the pursuit
to denounce the slave trade. In 1841 he presided over the
case of the escaped slaves who mutinied on the Amistad.
He also was a Whig in the 1820' and 1830's. He fought
against Jacksonian Democrats as a conservative Republican.

In 1829 he moved to Cambridge to become Harvard's first Dane Professor of Law. In 1845 he dies in Cambridge.

Could of Judge Joseph Story plot the murder of the elderly Captain Joseph White to remove his influence on his nephews and implicate his rivals the Crowninshields in the murder? He would accuse his brother-in-law Stephen White also of the murder. Captain Joseph White was bludgeoned and then stabbed 13 times. Could there had been two murderers? One who beat him with a club and killed him. The second who was not aware of the first who stabbed him 13 times. When Captain White was found dead his sheets were amazingly clean for someone who was stabbed 13 times with a dirk.

I have not been in these tunnels of yet. I have one friend who grew up in this home and several who had played with him and ran through the tunnel that leads from this house. Since I have seen that both of the White brother's house were connected I would conclude their brother-in-law and partner's home would be connected as well. Also Story's neighbor Richard Gardener's (17 Winter Street on the corner of Pickman Street) brother John had built the home that Captain White was murdered in. The Gardener brothers were Commons Improvement subscribers.

You can see Judge Story's house to the left and Joseph "Jr." Whites home to the right. Their backyards formed a large compound. Below is a view inside the fence to the right.

2. John Fairfield House
104 Andrew Street

Built in 1805 for Captain John Fairfield. Fairfield had
owned ships with Jon Andrew and Samuel Archer 3rd
who builds the Archer Block which will be replaced by
the Franklin Building on the corner of Essex Street and
Hawthorne Boulevard. Also he had lived in the Mason
House. He will also own ships with Salem Commons
Improvement Fund subscribers William B. Parker, Jonathan
Gardener Jr., and Jonathan Mason (Fairfield will live in
the Mason House on Washington Square North in 1814
before it is moved). John Mack, Daniel Hathorne (Salem
Commons Improvement Fund subscriber who is lost at sea
in 1805), John Derby III (built the Derby-Pickman Block
on Derby Square and continues the tunnel building after his
brother Elias moves to Londonberry, N.H.), and William

Kimball were his captains. William Kimball will own the Kimball Block that burned down in 1899. The Gathering Church and Mud Puddle Toys reside there now. Plus I give tours of the tunnel entrances in that building quite regularly. John Fairfield moves to Londonberry, N.H. to tend to Elias Hasket Derby Jr.'s sheep in 1814. He also was one of a few subscribers who paid twice when funds fell short for the Salem Commons Improvement Fund.

This home is one of a few that have exterior chimneys lining up on Andrew Street. I have not been able to enter this basement as of yet. Looking forward to it though....

3. Cook-Kimball House
14 Pickman Street

Built circa. 1807-1808 for Robert Cook Jr. who was a local painter. His father Robert Cook married Elizabeth Liscomb. He was a fisherman & mariner. They had 6 children; Elizabeth, Robert Jr., Benjamin, John Morong, and Martha. He married Hannah Gowan in 1800. Robert Cook Jr. son John Morang Cook was also a painter. Robert Cook Jr. has the wooden house to the right also built in 1813. Samuel Field McIntire builds both of them. The first home remained in the hands of Robert's heirs till 1839 when Captain James S. Kimball bought it.

The basement as of yet has not been graced by my presence, but I assume that the home is connected to the tunnel for the Sewer line with manhole covers marked "S" go past this home. Also the Mack Industrial School for Girls and the David Lord House next door are made out of brick. This brick would be needed to fork the tunnel up Collins Street to Barton Street where the tunnels continue through the backyards on the old Captain William B. Parker lots.

4. David Lord House
16 Pickman Street

Mason David Lord built this double house in 1817-1818 as a real estate venture. David Lord built the Andrew-Safford House and was one of the masons who worked on the Customs House on Derby Street. The exterior chimneys on this house line up with the two homes built by Robert Cook Jr. to the right.

I have not been in this basement as of yet, but give me time...

5. Mack Industrial School for Girls
17 Pickman Street

At the time of her death in 1884, Esther C. Mack made a bequest in her will for the erection of a school to provide employment training for women. In 1897 her friend Alfred Stone made her wish come true. With a committee of prominent Salem women Alfred Stone created the Mack Industrial School for Girls that by 1908 enrollment had grown to more than five hundred students. Young women between 14 and 18 could be trained to become a seamstresses or dressmakers' assistants enrolled in a twelve-month, five-day-a-week course. This was followed by a 3 month apprenticeship. The school also offered classes in millinery, embroidery, gardening, domestic skills, English, arithmetic, hygiene, and physical training. They also had accommodations to handle at least 70 Women at night.

Esther was the Secretary for the Dorcas Society as well. She also donated to the American Unitarian Church to establish the Harriet O. Mack Fund.

My only assumption that this house is connected by tunnel is its proximity to the other two brick buildings on this street and the line of manhole covers demarcated by "S". Then again deduction can lead you into strange places.

Cookbook from the Mack Industrial School for Girls.

6. William B. Parker House
33 Pleasant Street

William B. Parker built his home kitty corner of Parker
Court in 1851. Parker Court has the a tunnel running from
Winter street to the Isaac Smith House on the corner of
Pleasant and Bridge Streets. William Parker also owned
large tracts of land on March Street and lots composing of
Beacon (East Watson Street then) and Barton Streets. He
will own the Hawkes House for a short period too. The
E.W. Abbot House which will be described next was once
his property as well which is connected to the tunnels.

William Parker was the father of the Parker Brothers,

George and Charles, who started the toy company in the Franklin Building. William had owned ships with Joseph White Jr., John Andrews, and Benjamin Felt. He also was brought into a libel case in 1830 accusing Col. Upham as a Federalist smuggler during the Embargo Act (Report of Timothy Upham vs. Hill and Barton of New Hampshire Patriot and State Gazette). Hill and Barton also accused Upham of being a corrupt Collector of Customs in Portsmouth. The whole time Upham declared himself as much a Democratic-Republican as Crowninshield was. Remember the tunnels under George Crowninshield Sr.. house which became the Customs House in Salem...

When I first searched this basement in the first version of this book the deceased owner's son had the basement filled with large furniture after his mother's death. Then I returned during his estate sale and the basement was cleared out. Then I found the tunnel entrance had led under the granite stairs in the front of the house. This sealed entrance also had the usual raised cold sill. So it makes you wonder where the fortune started from that set up the Parker Brothers Toy company?

One of the games William's son would produce in Salem.

Games Made by the Parker Brothers

In the center there is one type of granite going from ceiling to floor. To the right there is a split of granite on the bottom and brick on top. We can also see the raised cold sill once more. This sealed entrance leads under the granite stairs in the front of the house.

7. E.W. Abbot House
4 Beacon Street

In 1871 the house was built on the old land that belonged
to William B. Parker for E. W. Abbot. William B. Parker
who was a ship captain who moved up to become the
president of the Naumkeag Bank which had resided in
the Bowker Building (Manning house), East India Marine
Hall, and the Asiatic Building. His wife Abigail was the
daughter of John Watson who was a school master in the
Union Building (Brown Building). The Watsons were
related through marriage to the Pickerings and Beacon Street
was once called East Watson Street. William Parker was the
father of the Parker Brothers who created Monopoly.

This property extended to Barton Street to Lathrop Street
on the east side of Bridge Street extending to the cove. Part

of the property on the sidewalk on Collins Street was sold to build a rail leading to the Eastern Railroad on Webb Street moving rail cars from the car manufacturer on Bridge Street where the brake and Clutch shop is now. For some time this house was a farm house that had the house to the left as its barn.

The tunnel entrance is in the rear of the basement under the stairs. Another entrance is in an old well on the back right corner which leads parallel to Beacon Street. I would assume this would connect to the sewer line on Barton Street. These tunnels were used by the Underground railroad to move runaway slaves through town. Ironic that the first 3 houses running up from the cove was built by the railroad to house their employees and William B. Parker sold part of the land to a railroad car manufacturer.

Also the house on the corner of Bridge Street was built in 1872 for Lucy Knight. The basement has sections of the concrete removed in front of a bulkhead entrance, but nothing more can be ascertained from it. These were the only houses on the road at the time.

The City Stables on Bridge Street once was a railroad car manufacture.

8. Thomas March Woodbridge House
48 Bridge Street at March Street

Built in 1809/1810 this house was built on 2 plots that Woodbrige and his wife Mary bought in 1801 and 1805. Being a bit of an oddity, this is the only McIntire House on Bridge Street. Most of Samuel McIntire's houses would be built on the waterfront, Commons, and Chestnut Street.

The house has 3 exterior chimneys. 1 runs in line with Bridge Street and two run with March Street. At the end of this road is where the original settlers lived. The Old Planters lived on the river on March Street overlooking the Old Sachem's wife village on the opposite shore. I have not been in here yet, but I will.... Captain White had partnered with the Cabots in Beverly which establishes a tie to this port between the two cities, was this the tunnel that linked the two centers? Plus the Cabot Farm has many secrets still to this day in North Salem...

9. Francis Skerry House
116 Bridge Street

Francis Skerry buys his first piece of property in Salem July 1670. In 1795 Ephraim Skerry inherits this lot from his father (Southern Essex County Registry Bk. 160 Pg. 16). John Saunders lived to the right, Thomas and Margaret Brown on Cross Street, and the rest stretched to the left to Lemon Street. Then Lemon Street was Smith Lane. Bridge Street was Ferry Lane. Cross Street was Brown Street. In 1801 master mariner Ephraim Skerry sells the lot to Samuel Buffum and John Howard (Southern Essex county Registry Bk. 168 Pg. 16) who were occupied as sail makers. Howard and Buffum were Salem Commons Improvement Fund subscribers. Then Benjamin Webb was their neighbor to the right. In 1810 John Howard sells to Richard Hay felt maker (Southern Essex County Registry Bk. 192 Pg. 156). By 1826

John Howard owns the lot once more and conveys it to his son Joseph Howard (Southern Essex County Bk. 242 Pg. 131). The deed lists a hat shop. At this time John Howard owns the right portion of the lot and John Howard Jr. owns the portion on Lemon Street. The hat shop now owned by Joseph Howard occupies the center portion. In 1827 Joseph Howard sells his portion to Aaron Endicott master mariner (Southern Essex County Registry Bk. 247 Pg. 68). Charles Endicott owns the lot in 1877 (Southern Essex County Registry Bk.990 Pg. 66), along with the old Brown estate on Cross Street. Charles sells it to Benjamin Creamer, who builds the Naumkeag Block which houses Pamplemousse today, in 1883 (Southern Essex County Registry Bk. 1109 Pg. 190). The lot on Cross Street was bought by Lewis Worthington ship carpenter (Southern Essex County Registry Bk. 199 Pg 141) from Margaret Brown after her husband Thomas died in 1813. Joseph Howard buys the Brown lot from Worthington in 1826 (Southern Essex County Registry Bk.199 Pg. 141) Today the lot occupying 2 Cross Street is under a separate deed from 116 Bridge Street.

Samuel Buffum and John Howard buy the house in the same year as Elias Hasket Derby Jr. begins the Salem Commons Improvement fund. The tunnel probably leads from the Isaac Smith House across the street on Pleasant. Also Benjamin Creamer buys the home later who built the Naumkeag Block that is also attached to the tunnels. This basement has the brick floor that can be seen in the White-Silsbee/Hodges-Mott House, White-Lord house, Francis Boardman House, and Naumkeag Block. There is one chimney towards the front that has along troth attached to it that might have had a staircase going down to the tunnel. The chimney in the back has a similar well that is also seen in the Pierce-Nichols House on Chestnut Street. Either could of led into the underground system in Salem.

This basement has areas where wood cover the brick floor. Could they be hiding entrances to a subbasement?

Could this troth been used to get sails into a tunnel through a covered stair below?

10. Isaac Smith House
121 Bridge Street at Pleasant Street

The lot was bought in 1798 from Cornelius and Grace Bartlett. The home was built in 1800 and Isaac lived in the home a short time before he died at sea in Jamaica at 33 in 1802. He was a Mason. His wife Elizabeth lived in it till 1804. He owned one ship, the Hiram, that was registered in Salem or Beverly with Nemiah Adams in which he captained and died on. His partner sells his share in the Hiram to Nathaniel Archer. In 1804 his wife sells it.

The tunnel runs through the fireplace arch on the last ell facing the Commons. Funny thing though, there was never a fireplace above this arch. The tunnel points towards Winter Street through a succession of backyards. There is also a deep hole that could of once had access to a trapdoor into the tunnel in front of the arch. The usual sewer lines can be found in the hole.

This arch is curious since there was never a chimney above it. This tunnel points across a vacant lot stretching behind 3 houses and across Parker Court to a home on Winter Street.

11. Samuel C. Clark House
5 Winter Street

The home was built in 1839 by Samuel C. Clark who was a painter.

Where the furnace was you can see the original brick floor. The rest of the basement floor had been cemented over. A similar floor to that of the Francis Skerry House and the Stephen and Joseph Jr. White Homes. The fireplace arch in the corner facing the Commons on Essex street is sealed closed. It is an external chimney. It could quiet possible had a trap door leading up into the arch. This chimney lines up to the one on the front left of 7 Winter Street.

12. William Safford House
11 Winter Street

In 1794 William Safford, a baker, sells to the wharfinger and
housewright Petaliah Brown (Registry of Deeds Title Book
157 Page 264 in 1794). William Safford owned 4 ships.
One with John Smith Then recorded in Book 162 Page 227.
Petaliah Brown buys the property behind him all the way to
Pleasant Street from Benjamin Pickman. The neighboring

lot to the right was owned by John Gardner.

Previous to 1846 Henry Tibbets buys the home from Jon Gardener. Tibbets was a customs inspector and Salem Commons Improvement Fund subscriber.

Then Petaliah Brown sells to Joseph Chipman Ward who was trader. Chipman owned the lot that the Naumkeag Block is on and the distillery and wharf on Front Street and Central Street. Ward would sell to Captain Edward H. Trumball.

The exterior chimneys on this property lines up with those on the Thomas Buxton House next door. Plus with John Gardner, William B. Parker, and Benjamin Pickman as neighbors, who are all Salem Common Improvement Fund subscribers, I am led to believe the tunnel path runs in front of this home if it is not connected. An added point of interest is that Petaliah becomes a wharfinger, Joseph Chipman Ward was a trader who had a tunnel running along Central Street from his distillery to the now Naumkeag Block, and Captain Edward H. Trumball was ship captain. All of them would have interest in the tunnels. The tunnel connected to this home might have been a commodity that increased the value of house which led to the trader and ship captain purchasing it?

13. Thomas Buxton House
7 Winter Street at Parker Court
(This side is now closed to traffic)

This house is deeded to Thomas Buxton in 1848. He
bordered the painter Samuel C. Clark on the left on Winter
and John Kinsman behind Clark on Parker Court. John
Kinsman was superintendent of the Eastern railroad when
the train tunnel was built through Washington Street.
William B. Parker also owned the Hawkes House on Derby

which was Elias Hasket Derby's privateering warehouse. He also owned the lot that 4 Beacon Street sits on with the tunnel used to transport runaway slaves. The Chimney on the back left lines up with the tunnel entrance on the Isaac Smith House on Pleasant and Bridge Streets. To this day there is not a single house built through this course of the tunnel. It is a collection of backyards and a large parking lot. Not one foundation has been dug to disturb its path.

Another friend of mine used to play in the tunnel leading from this house as a kid.

The chimney in the middle lines up with the Isaac Smith House on Pleasant Street. There is not one home built in between these two through the backyards.

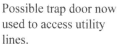

Possible trap door now used to access utility lines.

14. William Goodhue House
17 Winter Street and 3 Pickman Street

John Gardner originally owned the two lots that make up
the property on the western side of Pickman Street. A very
old Colonial residence of wood left by will in 1767 by
Jonathan Gardner Jr. to his son John, who built the Joseph
White house on Essex Street, stood on the corner of Winter
and Pickman Streets. Jonathan Gardner Jr. was the man
who petitioned the state to have the Salem Marine Society
incorporated in 1772. John Gardner had sold the property
that the Archer Block (Franklin Building) was to be built on
in 1809 to Samuel Archer 3rd . To the north stood another
very old wooden Colonial residence owned by Petaliah
Browne in which that genial antiquary the late Dr. Benjamin
F. Browne was born. He sold the southern half of the lot to

William Goodhue who built the current brick building on the corner of Winter and Pickman Street in 1805. Goodhue had owned the Kings Arm Tavern that would later be renamed the Sun Tavern after the Revolutionary War. The tavern was on the present location of the Bowker Block which houses the Peabody Essex Museum. William Goodhue sold the house and the estate which stretched from Winter to Pleasant Street on the western side of Pickman Street. In 1808 the master of the Salem East India Marine Society, Salem Commons Improvement Fund subscriber, and founding member of the second charter of the Essex Lodge Benjamin Carpenter owned the house and property (Southern Essex County Registry Bk 185 Pg 83) . Its entrance was on Pickman Street. This estate with its fine old fashioned New England garden marked off with high box borders into fragrant flower beds with here and there a tempting fruit tree extended the whole northern side of the western section of Pickman Street. Carpenter then sells to John Forrester (Southern Essex County Registry Bk 202 Pg 120).

The Northern lot was owned by Petaliah Browne. Dr. Benjamin Browne was born in that wooden house. Thomas Samson and James Brace owned the house before the Gardners. In 1811 Jon Gardner Jr. had this lot and the Gardner-Pingree House foreclosed upon. Captain Joseph White buys this house and the Gardener-Pingree House 3 years later from Nathaniel West. Captain Joseph White would be murdered in the Gardner-Pingree House. Captain Joseph White sells the house to John Forrester (Southern Essex County Registry Bk 196 Pg 252). Then William Parker buys the house.

The two lots become under one ownership in 1832. The southern brick house is sold to Adjutant General George

Humprey Devereux when he marries John Forrester's daughter in 1831. In 1832 William Parker sells the northern wooden house to Devereux. They changed hands again by one conveyance in 1841 and in 1849 both estates were sold to Henry Mellus who occupied the brick house not long after and replaced the old wooden house with a fine mansion of like material built for the occupancy of his brother in law Edward H Payson. In this new wooden house lived Francis Willoughby Pickman during his last stay in Salem.

Now when Jonathan Gardner Jr., John Gardner, William Goodhue, Benjamin Carpenter, Joseph White, and John Forrester have all lived in the brick house built in 1808, it has to have tunnels connecting to it. John Forrester had built the Forrester-Peabody House (Bertram House for Men on the Commons) in 1819 and buys the brick house on Pickman in 1831 a year after Captain Joseph White's murder. In 1834 he sells the Forrester-Peabody House which was connected to the tunnels. Captain Joseph White was murdered in the Gardner-Pingree House. The culprit escaped through the tunnels from that home. Benjamin Carpenter was a merchant who was the Master of the Salem East India Marine Society, founder of the 2nd Essex lodge, and Salem Common Improvement subscriber who would find the house useful for storing cargo before it reaches the stores on Essex Street. William Goodhue could of stored liquor from distilleries that smuggled molasses to sell in his Sun Tavern which the Peabody Essex Museum used the tunnels to travel from their offices to the museum. John Gardner the 2nd had built the Gardner-Pingree House which Captain Joseph White was murdered in. So how can the brick house not be connected to the tunnels? At 2 Pickman Street was the brick house occupied during his residence in Salem by the Rev. William Bawlins Pickman. On the southern corner of Winter Street stood a wooden dwelling now moved back to 4 Pickman Street. These homes need to be further researched.

Downtown

-Chapter 4-

Downtown

So here is the climax of our narrative and also of the
tunnels. This is where the money was made. Here was
where the politics of the city happened in taverns,
city offices, and secret societies. This is the place the
goods were smuggled into to be sold in shops lining
this area and their proceeds snuck into the basements
of the vaults of various banks. Bisecting this area is
the train tunnel that had a secret station inside for
judges and special prisoners to be delivered to the
court house on Federal Street. The train tunnel with
the lost secret track.

There were 7 wharfs stretching on what is New
Derby Street now and one on Washington Street. The
ship mechanics were where the Post Office is now in
what was called "Knockers Hole" from the sound of
all of the hammers.

It has seen state sponsored murders with those
accused of witch craft and the most notorious murder
on the nineteenth century. It had the wealthiest men
in the country walk it from the 1600's to the late
1800's. The "Old Planters" who established this town
would move off March Street and plan their house lots
that ran either side of Essex Street stretching either
to the North River or the South River. Washington
Street was an old Native path that led to the ancient
well on Washington and Essex Street. Churches even
had tunnels running into them! Tunnels ran through
jails, courts, city halls, stores, banks, taverns, secret

societies, museums, libraries, private homes and churches!

The Derby family had several mansions here. Ezekiel Derby had a mansion on Essex Street. His father had two mansion that succeeded each other. One on Washington Street where the current Mason building is now and another where Old Town Hall is. His son Elias Hasket Jr. would live there for ten years as he dug a new leg of tunnels through town for those Common Improvement Fund subscribers.

Joseph Peabody had his wharf next to the old hospital where the Salem Housing Authority has its office and high rise on Charter Street. His house was donated so the Armory could be built on it. He merged several museums together and helped them build the East India Marine Hall which is attached to the Peabody Essex Museum.

This area had lectures by learned men such as Charles Lenox Remond, Fredrick Douglass, Sarah Parker Remond, John Quincy Adams, Henry Longfellow, Oliver Wendell Holmes, and Henry David Thoreau. Alexander Graham Bell invented and made his first public display of the telephone here. Brigham Young heard of the murder of Joseph Smith in a house here. Presidents, Washington, Monroe, Madison, Jackson, and John Quincy Adams have attended banquets in this part of town. Plus the first armed interaction in the Revolutionary War occurred here!

Plus many of the houses are haunted! Well the whole town is haunted, this is just the section that has been on T.V. shows and in numerous books....

Washington Street towards the train station above and the Lawrence Block below on Front Street. Two main corridors of commerce and smuggling in the 1800's.

1. Gardner Pingree House
128 Essex Street

Built in 1804-1805 for John Gardener Jr. by Samuel
McIntire. Jeremiah Page provided bricks, David Robbins
was the mason, Joseph Fogg the lumber, Epes Cogswell was
housewright, and William Luscoomb III painter. Gardner
had owned 6 ships. All but 2 had different captains and
co-owners. He never captained any of his ships. The only
economic venture he went on twice with anyone was with
his relative Simon Gardener who had owned two ships
with him and captained both. Next door was the site of the
Captain Joseph Gardener home where the Plummer Hall
now stands that houses the Essex Institute. The Captain was
killed by Narragansetts in 1675 at the Great Swamp Fight.
At the Captain's death his wife Anne inherited her father's

Emmanuel Downing's house which is west of Plummer Hall and married Gov. Simon Bradstreet and lived there. This house was torn down in 1750 and Francis Peabody built his mansion. This book was written across the street from where the first American poet wrote her books, Anne Bradstreet.

In 1811 John Gardner Jr. ran into financial problems and sold the house to Nathaniel West. Nathaniel West was a captain who owned many ships with Nehemiah Andrews, Crowninshields, Derbys, Benjamin Pickman, and Francis Boardman. Nathaniel West bought the John Turner mansion, next to the Peter Palfrey House to the right, opposite Central Street in 1833 and opened it as a tavern called "The Mansion house" in time for President Andrew Jackson's visit. Later it would be called the "West Block". Nathaniel West sold it three years later to Captain Joseph White. He was murdered in this house.

It's raining, it's pouring.
The old man is snoring.
He went to bed bumped his head,
and he couldn't get up in the morning."

Captain Joseph White who bought the "Come Along Patty" from Elias Haskett Derby with the Cabot brothers and renamed it the "Revenge" became the first privateer from Salem. He was in the slave trade. He had questionable feelings towards a young niece who lived with him. He hated the man whom she would marry and made a fortune which he was not going to give her any. In the winter of 1829-1830 Captain Joseph White was feeling ill and had his lawyer Joseph Waters draft him a new will. In 1830 someone snuck through the tunnel and murdered him. Not just once, but possibly on 3 separate occasions.

This murder would inspire Edgar Allen Poe's to write the Tell Tale Heart. It is reminiscent of Agatha Christies's Murder on the Oriental Express. The intrigue of the murder and the sudden death of Judge Parker might of led Parker Brothers to buy the U.S. rights to the 1949 Cluedo/Clue game because it reminded them of the strange tale that happened in this Salem house! I wonder if it was a literature fan who moved the Crowninshield-Bentley House to the right from its old home in the Hawthorne Hotel's parking lot. That house was in H.P. Lovecraft's story "The Thing on the Doorstep". Also Rev. Bentley wrote his memoirs of Salem in the Crowninshield-Bentley House.

Captain Joseph White was not kind to his relations that had worked for him in his house. He only showed a special form of kindness to his young attractive niece. The announcement of her engagement to a captain that was just released from Joseph Jr. & Stephen White Co.'s employment just sent him into a furor. At 82 he is abandoned by his niece and is ill during a hard winter. His favorite nephew has been dead for some years but his brother is still at the old captain's side. Was Stephen jealous of the attention his uncle gave to his female cousin or the attention she deprived him? Did Stephen foster some hatred towards his uncle for favoring his dead brother over him? Did the old Captain plan a mercy killing that would blame the Knapps of murder to remedy the capture of a ship he once owned?

We will not know, but we do know who ever snuck into to kill the old man knew of the tunnels. The tunnels connect the White/Story compound to the old man's mansion. The old man bankrolled Joseph Jr. & Stephen White Co. and the construction of his nephews houses with the tunnels attached

to them. I have been in the White brothers homes and seen
the sealed up entrances to the tunnels and I have friends who
have played in the tunnels attached to Judge Story's House.
I have been in the tunnels under the old Sacon Jewelry
Building. It leads me to strongly believe that this house
with exterior chimneys, the tunnel marked on an old city
engineers map leaving the Armory, it was built by Samuel
McIntire, plus manhole covers reading "Sewer", "Drain",
and "S" this house is connected to the tunnels in town.

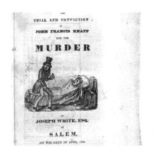

2. Wynott Wands
127 Essex Street

This building is haunted. A brother and sister died here in a fire and have not moved on to their paradise. The little girl will lure women into a false sense of security over a series of weeks and then turn on them. At least one woman has had a nervous breakdown with several others vowing never to go down those steps again. The older brother who was of a large built was mentally deficient before his death. He will make attempts to communicate with those he feels comfortable with. When he is frustrated with his inability

to communicate with those he trusted he has been known
to throw ceiling panels across the room and to disturb the
surface of various desks within the basement in a tantrum.
He has since left to better places along with his sister.

Also this basement housed a hair salon that would do
the hair of cancer patients and corpses for the local funeral
homes. It was a private salon out of the view of public
scrutiny. An air of misery lingers within these walls and
seeps through a wall of sheet rock that hides the access to
the tunnels on Essex Street.

Paranormal detectives and ghost hunter associations and
T.V. shows flock here. As you walk through their doors, you
might wonder what strange occurrences might befall you... I
hope you live. Plus it is the new office of Salem House Press
and studio of Chris Dowgin.

3. Gideon Tucker House
129 Essex Street

Built in 1818-1819 by Samuel McIntire for Gideon Tucker. He was a merchant who had owned several ships with his neighbor Joseph Peabody. This house resembled Captain White's house across the street before the Father Matthew Catholic Total Abstinence Society remodeled it in 1910. The society bought the house in 1896. The original neoclassical rounded porch is now on the rear of the Plummer Hall across the street.

Father Theobald Matthew was an Irish priest who in 1838 believed that one enduring act would keep a person sober for life. Half of Ireland enrolled into his society before he came to America to spread the society abroad. In 1849 Congress admitted him within the bar of the Senate, an honor only

General Lafayette had received previously. In September of that year he visited Salem. In 1887 a statue of him was erected on the corner of Charter and Central Street (opposite the old Police Station) near an old well opposite R. Stone's distillery (Murphys and previously Roosevelt's). The well was open to run off from the street and became as poisonous as Father Matthew thought alcohol was. In 1916 the statue was moved to the park in between Hawthorne Blvd. and Vine Street at the corner of Derby Street. The statue stands opposite the Lydia Pinkham Memorial on New Derby Street. Lydia Pinkham created a slew of mother's little helpers which allowed women during prohibition to get drunk legally with her patent medicine. Ironic.

I am not sure beyond if this building has tunnels leading to it beyond the fact the tunnel runs past it, Gideon Tucker was partners with Joseph Peabody, and it was built by Samuel McIntire.

Father Theobald Matthew

4. Tucker Daland House
132 Essex Street Right

Built in 1851 after moving a house to Washington and
Bridge Street to be used as a city orphanage called Looby
Asylum built by Charles Bulfinch. Plus we all know
Bulfinch loved tunnels... John Tucker Daland was married
to Captain Thomas Whittredge's daughter who was a
Salem Common Improvement Fund subscriber. Daland
resigned from the Merchant's Bank which Crowninshield
was president of to join the board of the Asiatic Bank
with Stephen White as its first president. The Asiatic Bank
would first be housed in the East India Marine Hall which
Steven White had built. He created the East India Marine
Hall Corporation to build the Marine Hall across from his
boyhood home on Essex Street in 1824.

John Tucker Daland had owned many ships along

with Joseph Peabody, Thomas Perkins, George Peabody, Benjamin Pickman, John L. Gardner, Robert Stone, Thomas Whitteridge, and Henry T. Daland. Many of these merchants were subscribers of the Salem Commons Improvement Fund. This along with two exterior chimneys running parallel to Essex Street and one heading directly to an exterior chimney placed dead center close to the front of the house on Brown Street. The former tunnel runs through a large yard with nothing built upon it.

5. Plummer Hall
132 Essex Street Left

Built in 1857 by a donation from Miss Caroline Plummer for the Salem Athenaeum in 1854 in memory of her brother Ernestus Augustus Plummer. The athenaeum rented the first floor to the Essex Institute. The Essex Institute was founded in 1848 when the Essex Historical Museum (formed in 1821) merged with the Essex Natural History Museum (1833). Dr. Edward Augustus Holyoke was the Essex Historical Museum's first president when he was close to 100 years old. Dr. A. Nichols of Danvers founded the other. After their merger Hon. Daniel A. White served as their new president. In 1867 George Peabody had donated $140,000 to house the natural history portion of the institute in a grand setting. Then in 1992 the Essex Institute merged with the Peabody Academy of Science to become the Peabody Essex Museum.

Plummer Hall was built for the Salem Athenaeum and they remained there till they built a smaller building at 337 Essex Street in 1906. The Salem Athenaeum was founded in 1810 when the Social and Philosophical libraries merged. The Social Library was founded in 1760 by Dr. Edward Augustus Holyoke. The Philosophical Library was founded in 1781 when a privateer captured a ship which housed the library of the celebrated Dr. Richard Kirwan as they crossed the Irish Canal. The library bought these books in Beverly and added them to their collection. The Salem Athenaeum was first stored in the Central Building (Trolley Depot). Later it would be stored in Essex Place, above the Salem Bank on the site of the Downing Block (Samantha's Costume Shop) in 1825, Lawrence Place (Bleachers and now Roost) in 1841, and then Plummer Hall in 1857. They sold Plummer Hall outright to the Essex Institute.

The building sits on part of the estate of Emmanuel Downing who came here in 1636. Emmanuel Downing was a barrister from the Inner Temple of London, a building that was leased from the Knights of the Templars till 1312. His daughter marries Governor Bradstreet and becomes one of America's first poets. This house was torn down in 1750. Also the Nathaniel Reed (Inventor of the Paddle Boat) House in which Captain Joseph Peabody lived in was built on this site. His son Francis Peabody had a mansion to the left.

I have not been in this building's basement but it is connected to the Tucker Daland House next door. Many of the Essex Institute's members were subscribers of the Salem Common Improvement Fund. The other indicator is that Captain Joseph Peabody had a home on this site. When they tear down a house they keep the original basement and add to it when necessary, tunnel and all.

6. Armory of the Salem Cadets
136 Essex Street

This was the residence of Col. Francis Peabody built in 1818 on portion of Governor Simon Bradstreet's estate. Originally this home was built by Captain Joseph Peabody for his son Joseph Augustus. The Peabody's house was the front section of the armory which has since been demolished and a park has been erected in its place. In 1890 the Stephen Abbot Associates of Cadets purchased the house and added the drill shed which is 86 feet long by 9 feet wide. The

Second Corps of Cadets first commander was Stephen Abbott in 1786. This corps would train several officers for the military. The portion of the armory in Peabody's house had a fine banquet hall which entertained Prince Arthur of England upon the death of London banker George Peabody in 1870. George Peabody formed the banking firm of George Peabody and Company which would later merge with Junius Spencer Morgan (J.P. Morgan's father) to form Peabody, Morgan, and Company. Morgan Greenfell (now part of Deutsche Bank), J.P. Morgan and Chase, and Morgan Stanley. J.P. Morgan and Chase and Morgan Stanley would be part of the 2008 bailout along with Alexander Hamilton's Bank of New York. Peabody would create several museums and institutes including the Peabody Academy of Science which is now the Peabody Essex Museum. The Armory of the Salem Light Infantry was in the Franklin Building (site of the Hawthorne Hotel). The house was razed in 1908. Some of the original woodwork survives in the Mason Lodge on Washington Street.

In 1908 the Company H, Eight Regiment, Massachusetts Volunteer Militia would build a new castle like armory to share with the Second Corps of Cadets. Company H was the Salem Light Infantry which was housed in the Franklin Building. The Salem Light Infantry was founded in 1805. FDR stopped here during a campaign tour to attend a ball. After WWII the armory was headquarters for the First Battalion, 102d Field Artillery. They remained here up till 1982 when a series of fires on Halloween burnt down the Cadet House on the front of the Armory. The Battalion moved to Lynn.

These tunnels can be confirmed on old engineer maps that were in the City Hall Annex on Washington Street. The tunnel was used to transport black powder from the seawall on New Derby Street. The map is now missing. Steve Dibble confirmed this for me. He was the city engineer for a period of time. Also you can still see the tunnel across the street from the armory. There are two square utility access holes which you can peer into. You will see a brick shaft in each going down 4 ft. till you see 4 granite lintels. Then the shafts drops down another 8 feet to brick floor. This is the next dog leg after the one in front of the Hawthorne Hotel.

Under Your Feet On Essex Street

From the basement of the old Sacon Jewelry store you can walk along the longest corridor of the tunnels. It is also one of the most mysterious.

Across the street is the Salem Armory. According to an old Salem Engineer, Steve Dibbel, there is indication of a tunnel leading from the Armory to the old seawall on New Derby Street below the old Burial Point on a city engineers map. The engineer map is now missing! Torn out of the book. The tunnel was used to transport black powder. You still can look down into this portion of the tunnels through two rectangle open metal grates. It seems to be one of the many dog legs and possible a major crossroad that would of ran under New Liberty Street which the Peabody Essex Museum stole for their expansions. These chambers have four granite lintels supporting 5 feet of bricks above. Then the floor of these chambers are seven feet lower.

The building right next to it is the old Sacon Jewelry Store which houses 13 Ghosts. Sacon Jewelry was opened by Mr. Van Dell who was an Italian from Argentina who

changed his name because it sounded too much like Sacco who was recently executed as an anarchist when he moved to America. His store was on the site of the Joshua Grafton House. Joshua lived there with his wife Hannah and their 3 kids. Grafton was a shipmaster. Capt. Joseph Peabody lived in this home before he moved across the street to the Reed Home where Plumer Hall is now.

In the nineties the owner of Black Cat Bookstore (which was the storefront Mr. Van Dell leased to the left of his jewelry store in his building) had walked into the tunnel from the basement and made it half way to the Peabody Essex Museum. Roughly 4 years ago construction crews were doing work in front of the building. Many people questioned the workers and police if it had to do with the tunnels. One officer was quite irate and told my friend there is no tunnels in town. In fact utility works are trained to deny any tunnels within seaport towns... Once I entered this basement I found out what really happened.

When you visit this basement and walk toward Essex Street things become strange. The first thing you notice is that whole wall fronting Essex Street has been replaced. Brand new water mains have been installed, but the size of this installation does not justify replacing the whole wall! Then you look up. They replaced the corrugated steel that supports the sidewalk above. Yes, I have walked out of the basement and into the tunnel. There are people walking above my head! Later you will read about the corrugated steel in front of the Samuel Ward Lot that supports the pedestrian walkway. Unfortunately theirs is rotting through, so be careful walking in front of the building... Also in the ceiling there are large metal squares with round cut piece of glass inserted into them. These plates brought light into the tunnels. When Puritans moved to create Salem in Oregon they brought their penchant for building tunnels. To this day you still can see people walking through the tunnels through these plates at night as their flashlights pass by. In this picture you can see where the plate met the wall. Also notice what remains of the old wall. The most interesting question that arises is, what was on the other side of this wall? Joseph Peabody had lived in the homes on either side of the street and he was one of this town's most lucrative smugglers? His son would own the property the Armory is on. Could there be a large chamber running from these three houses under Essex Street? Who knows.

Now if you turn right from the new wall and walk to the corner you will find new brick sealing the tunnel walkway toward the Hawthorne Hotel. Testimony to this can be seen in the picture that started this section. Then to the right of that along the alley there is a cubby hole with a grate above it that once had access to the pavement above.

The strangest section is in the middle which has a closed room with small vents leading into it. It has three outlets into it and has a 4 foot raised floor.

Then if you turn around and head back down the new wall and head to the Peabody Essex Museum you will find the sealed entrance that the bibliophile had ventured through. She complained that the tunnel was quite damp. Could of it been from a busted water main that went unnoticed for years? Then to the left of that is another strange cubby which was filled with granite rubble. All in all this building has acquired the largest amount of the tunnel in town to expand their basement space. The owner who did the original work must of known of the tunnels to have enough faith to tear down the wall and find the tunnel on the other side. Was it a member of the Peabody family?

Then if you leave this basement and go into the basement of the oldest section of the building there was some of those arches seen in many of the houses in this book.

Well this building s only second to the building that the Naumkeag Trust/ Eastern Bank was in (on the Samuel Ward Lot) for having the most secrets. It holds the largest section of the tunnel in town, even if none of it beyond the plates in the ceiling are original. It is even longer than the section leaving the Daniel Lowe building. Even in the Daniel Lowe building its tunnel was rehabbed in somewhere between 1874 and 1918.

Sealed Entrance heading toward Peabody Essex Museum.

Corrugated Steel ceiling holding up the sidewalk.

Cubby Hole above to the left of the sealed tunnel entrance heading toward the museum.

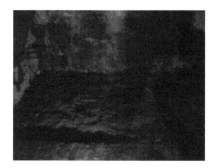

Strange hole in the floor.

7. Bowker Block
144-156 Essex Street

The vicinity of the Bowker Block was home to one of the many taverns on what is now the pedestrian walkway. From the head of St. Peter Street to Central Street was the Old Planter Peter Palfrey's estate. On this site there was several taverns throughout history.

Starting on Essex Street across from Trolley Depot on Essex Street was John Gedney's Ship Tavern in 1692. John Stacy would run it before the year was out. Then in 1693 Francis Ellis ran it. In the early 18th century this was the most noted tavern in town. It was torn down in 1740. Then John Turner built his mansion on the spot in 1748. He sold it to Judge Andrew Oliver who sold it to Nathaniel West. In 1833 it was reopened as a tavern called the Mansion House.

Then on the site of the Bowker Block was another tavern.
It was built on the William Browne estate (1698). It was
said a vast sum of New England Shillings was buried in the
chimney during the Dutch Wars and was found by his heir
Col. Benjamin Brown upon his marriage in 1730. But before
it was a tavern it was William Gray's first mansion.

In 1770 William Goodhue opened the Kings Arm Tavern
on the site that the Salem Five Savings Bank is on now.
During the Revolutionary War it became the Sun Tavern.
Samuel Robinson bought it from him who sold it to
Benjamin Webb. In 1792 the Hatter's shop across from
it burned down with another home on the site of the old
Eastern Bank on the Samuel Ward Lot. Widows Beckford
and Manning died in these homes. In 1899 this lot would
see another fire while it was used as a bank. Also in 1792
a dinner was held at the Sun Tavern for the reopening of
Essex Mason Lodge. His son Jonathan Webb sells the
property to William Gray who tears the building down in
1800 and builds a new mansion there. The Sun Tavern was
moved to his old mansion where the Bowker Block is and
reopens the Sun Tavern in 1800. In 1814 Prince Stetson
bought the mansion and opened the Essex Coffee House.
After General Lafayette stopped here it was named the
Lafayette Coffee House for a very brief time. In 1842 it was
the Essex House.

William Gray's old mansion was on the current site of
the Peabody Essex Museum offices within the Bowker
Block. William Gray was a merchant who became a senator
supported by the Federalist in town. During the French
Revolution those who supported it became Jacobins of the
Republican party. The Federalists mocked them by calling
them Democrats. When the Federalists lost the power in

their name they became Republicans which became Whigs. William Gray was a senator who supported Jefferson's Embargo Act. This proved so unpopular he was forced to move to Boston in 1809 where he became Lieutenant Governor. He started his career in the services of Richard Derby the grandfather of Elias Hasket Derby Jr. .

In 1805 William Gray sold the building to Union Marine Insurance Company. William Manning then ran the Sun tavern in the building. It also housed the Post Office and the Naumkeag Bank. The Sun Tavern closes in 1828. Then in 1830 another building was built on this site. It was called the Bowker Block and was built by the mason William Roberts. William Roberts built the home on the corner of Washington Square and Winter, Saint Peter's Church, and the East India Marine Hall which had tunnels running from them. The storefront was added in 1894. The Second Corp of Cadets, the local police court, and the Merchant Bank had tenures in here as well. This was also where Almy's and Filene's had their first department stores. In 1975 L.H. Rogers rehabilitated the block and created a woman's clothing store there.

After the East India Mall and the Bowker Block was refitted and the covered walkway on the two buildings converted it into retail space the Peabody Essex Museum bought it to house their offices. They used the tunnels up to recently to travel back and forth to the museum. Now one of them is being used as a vault.

8. East India Marine Hall
161 Essex Street

Built in 1825 from the creation of the East India Marine
Hall Corporation founded by Stephen White was the current
president of the Salem East India Marine Society. The
mason who built it was William Roberts. The Salem East
India Marine Society was founded in 1799 by supercargoes
and ship captains who have rounded the Cape of Good
Hope and Cape Horn. The hall would be built across
from Stephen White's boyhood home and counting house.
Benjamin Hodges was the societies first president as well as
master of the Essex Lodge. The museum was incorporated
in 1801 to house objects gathered by their members from
their sea voyages to create a museum of curiosities. Upon
the East India Marine Hall's opening John Quincy Adams

presided over banquet. On the first floor was the Asiatic Bank, the post office, and the Oriental Insurance Company. The two companies were founded by Stephen White. In 1867 the hall was refitted by donations from George Peabody who was the London banker in business with J.P. Morgans father.

The Essex Historical Institute, The Essex Natural History Museum, East India Marine Museum, and the Peabody Academy of Science have been combined to make the Peabody Essex Museum. The hall has been added onto from 1885 to 2000 on various sides. In 2013 it will see future expansion. The museum now holds collections of Chinese, Korean, Japanese, Oceanic, Indian, Native American art along with collections of portraits, furniture, and maritime history from Essex County. For over 300 years this society has been collecting things from around the world. They have vaults in basements and subbasements under the East India Marine Hall and the Armory. I do not believe we will ever see the true extant of their collections. What fabulous items have they smuggled through the tunnels from the sea? There is rumors they have the Romanov crown jewels, Blackbeard's skull, religious artifacts, and magical items from around the world stored in their vaults.

This is the ruin of Benjamin Pickman's estate before it was torn down. It resided to the right of the East India Marine Hall set back from the street. In front of it would reside Pickman Place.

More photographs of the Benjamin Pickman Estate.

9. Downing Block
173-175 -177 Essex Street

Built in 1858 for dry good merchants Thomas W. Downing
and John Downing on the site of Pickman Place. In 1803
the Salem Bank and the Salem Marine Insurance Company
resided on the first floor of Pickman Place. Its presidents
included Benjamin Pickman and Joseph Peabody. In 1804
the Salem East India Marine Society Museum resided at
Pickman Place. The Essex Historical Society which is now
part of the Peabody Essex Museum was above the Salem
Bank in that building. In 1818 the Institute for Savings in
the Town of Salem and Vicinity occupied the building. This
was founded by Edward Augustus Holyoke. It was known as
the Salem Bank. In 1830 there was an attempt to break into

the their vault. Dr. Edward Holyoke, Benjamin Pickman, Timothy Pickering, Benjamin Crowninshield, Daniel A. White, and Nathaniel Silsbee were members. In 1843 the bank changed its name to the Salem Savings Bank. In 1844 the Salem Savings Bank will move into Pickman Place. The Essex County Natural History Museum was housed here when it merged with the Essex Historical Society to become the Essex Institute in 1848.

In 1869 the Salem Fraternity which is the oldest boy's club in the country was founded within the new Downing Block. It was created to create evening instruction and wholesome amusement for those "who were confined to their work during the day who needed recreation at the end of their labors". Physical training, general education, and arts and crafts were offered. They had a library, a reading room, and amusement room. These services were provided to boys and girls for free. In 1899 the Salem Fraternity buys the Joshua Phippen Essex Bank Building on Central Street. After being housed their they merge with other national clubs to become the Boys & Girls Club. Their current Salem location is in the hall next to the Immaculate Conception Church.

This building has a curious set of tunnels. Under the entrance that leads to the stairs to the 2nd and 3rd floors is a long hall way in the building. On the back of the building in this hall is an iron door covered in thick glass. At this point the long sliding latch is rusted shut. I was able to pull the doors hinges free from the wall, but the concrete wall behind it is well mortared. From this point to the front are several arches on the left and right. In one arch you can look through a hole and look into the basement under the old Samantha's Costume Shop. Before you get to the stairs

there are a pair of metal doors. These open into rooms on
either side of the hallway. Two shoots can be seen entering
them from the ceiling. Behind the stairs is the original
neon sign for Bernard's Jewelers . Past the stairs there are
arches with old furnace doors in them. Then right before
the Essex Street entrance to the tunnel there are a pair of
arches with doors in them. The one to the left has a mail
slot in the bottom of it. On the other side of this door is a
metal bracing composed of a series of "x"s. In this room
the tunnel entrance extends 5 feet into the basement. In the
other arch opposite of this is another door that leads to the
basement under Witch T's. This storefront was once home
to the Goddess Treasure Chest. The Goddess Treasure Chest
resides in the old Daniel Low warehouse which has a tunnel
leading to it. Also her home in the Derby-Pickman Building
is also connected. Now the tunnel entrance to Essex Street
has been bricked closed, but there is a hole big enough to
climb through. This section of tunnel was filled with ash
and pumice which has caved in from the right and the left.
Above is a granite slab which you can see in the sidewalk
in front of the door. The corridor is about 3 feet wide and 7
feet tall. Roots were growing through the tunnel from the
direction of the Hawthorne Hotel. The tunnel extended past
the granite slab and had water pipes running through it.
Soon after the first printing of this book the Peabody Essex

Museum buys this building
to protect their secrets.

Middle of the original tunnel that
ran between the two sections of
Pickman Place.

The Arches

Sealed Arches under Turtle Alley in the Downing Building. My guess is the tenants of this building that needed multiple arches were those connected to the Salem Bank/Salem Savings Bank. For they will have similar arches constructed in the basement of the building that stands on the Samuel Ward lot. The difference here is that there is three rows of arches before you get the next building which was part of Pickman Place.

It was rumored that Runaway Slaves were hidden behind these arches in sleeping compartments waiting for the next leg of their journey. Now sealed up with what looks like a stove flu sticking out of it.

In this sealed compartment you can now see a flu and stove opening. Is this the back of the compartment? Did each of them have their own stove to warm its guests?

The Doors

This the door in the front arch off of the Essesx Street Tunnel under Witch T's.

This door across from the one above even had its own mail slot below the mustache.

Essex Street Tunnel

Inside

This is under the granite block just outside of the central corridor that allows entrance to the offices on the top floors. Unfortunately it was sealed on both sides with creosote from the furnaces.

The Tunnel with the Arches

Looking from Essex Street down the tunnel.

The Author looking at the Iron Door sealing access to the Charter Street tunnel.

Behind the iron bars were two plate glass pieces about an inch thick each. Behind that was new cinder block. To the left you can see the doors near the Essex Street entrance.

Looking from Charter Street at the stairs.

The stairs to the central corridor above.

Two angles on a strange room behind a metal door with a chute entering it from above.

10. Naumkeag Block
185-189 Essex Street and 1 Central Street

Built in 1847 by Benjamin Creamer. Had once belonged to
John Derby and stretched from Essex Street along Central
Street to the South River on Front Street to his wharf and
distillery. John Derby sells the lot to Captain Joseph White
and Robert Stone. They sell to Joshua Phippen who in turn
sells the lot to Joseph Chipman. Joshua Phippen developed
the lot on which the Essex Bank Building was on. Joseph
Chipman was one of the owners of the William Safford
House at 11 Winter Street that has a tunnel running to Isaac
Smith's house. Joshua Phippen erected a store on the lot that
Ana Phippen ran during Chipman's tenure previous to 1803.
Benjamin Dodge buys the lot next and has his store here. In
1831 The Naumkeag Bank moves in which was connected

to the Naumkeag Steam Mills which both had Edward Kimball as president. Edward Kimball would be president of the Salem Five Cents Savings Bank in 1855 too. Before Dodge sells the lot in 1835 there is brick store next to the Pickman Estate, a wooden dwelling, and brick stores on the corner of Essex and Central Street with outbuildings. The deed always gives right to land under and adjoining the lot. Was this a right for passage through the tunnel from Essex Street to the distillery on the wharf? Benjamin Dodge in 1835 sells the Brick building on the left to the lawyer Larkin Thorndike and the wooden dwelling, out buildings, and stores to the right to Benjamin Creamer. In 1847 Benjamin Creamer has the Naumkeag Block built on the lot.

The basement in this building has two foundations put together and exhibits floor boards in the rafters from the 1700's. There is a tunnel entrance on its left side if you are looking at the building from Essex Street. You can see a portal sealed by bricks. The foundation on either side is of a granite construction. Below this portal there is a hole in the floor about 3 ft by 5 ft sealed with brick. Similar to a hole in the building occupied by The Gathering Church in the floor inside the tunnel entrance. Also it shows a similar tunnel entranced sealed off leading to The Essex Bank on Central Street and to the old distillery and Wharf on the South River originally built for John Derby. After breaking through some sheet rock we found another tunnel entrance sealed off similar to the White-Lord house and in the building occupied by the Gathering Church.. The roof of this entrance had some old floor boards falling from the ceiling. This entrance led into the old Customs House next door. In the sidewalk on Central Street you can see the granite that housed a service entrance to the basement. The door still exists in the basement.

Entrance that leads to the Essex Bank. From near where I took this picture to my right was another entrance behind some sheet rock which was removed leading to the Trolley Depot across Central Street. It was just too dark to get a good picture. There is some interesting granite work in the sidewalk above this entrance

Detail of above.

In the front left corner of the basement is another sealed entrance. The access to the utilities has been bricked over.

The Tunnel leading down Central Street from the Naumkeag Block would terminate at the building at the end of the inlet on this wharf.

The tunnel stretched from Essex Street down Central Street to this wharf originally built for John Derby who also owned the lot that the Kimball Building sat on. Joseph White, Benjamin Dodge, and Robert Stone will own this wharf that was where Central Street is now.

Another sealed entrance to Essex Street. Above the printer you can see the cinder blocks used to seal the portal off. To the left and right is the original granite of the foundation.

11. Central Building
4-10 Central Street

Built in 1805 this block of stores was built for William Gray
Jr. and Benjamin Hathorne. Joseph McIntire and Samuel
McIntire had worked on the construction of this building.
William Gray Jr. had a mansion that sat where the Bowker
Block is and also built a later one where the Salem Five
Bank is now. His old house had 2 exterior chimneys.

William "Billy" Gray was a leading merchant of his day. He was one of the 5 millionaires in town; Elias Hasket Derby, Joseph White, Simon Forrester, and Joseph Peabody being the others. In 1801 the Federalist was in majority over the Democratic-Republicans within the richest families in town. In 1802 an association of Federalist put forth an act not to deal with the Republican Crowninshields which William Gray Jr. successfully opposed. William Gray Jr. was the fifth William. He had his name changed to William S. Gray. In 1807 William S. Gray was elected to the U.S. Senate. In 1807 following Napoleon's "Berlin Decree" ,which France tried blocking trade to British ports, the "Milan Decree" authorized French warships and privateers to capture neutral ships sailing from any British port or from any country that was occupied by British forces. It also declared that any ships that submitted to search by the Royal Navy on the high seas were to be considered lawful prizes if captured by the French. At the same time England ordered that any ship leaving U.S. would have to sail to a British port and pay duties before it ventured on to Europe. The only other port that U.S. was able to sail to was Sweden. In response to this Jefferson opted the Embargo Act on Dec. 22 1807 to halt all shipping from leaving U.S. Ports with very few exceptions. This was an attempt to force England to change its policies and straggle it economical by withholding American goods. William S. Gray supported this measure as being constitutional and now he was open game by the Federalists who elected him. In a letter to the Salem Gazette (August 1808) he supported his decision and admitted the act did cost him 10 percent of his wealth at the time. It was Mr. Gray's opinion that seizure of our ships by France or Britain was so great the Embargo Act was the only measure that would promise our sailors safety. The month preceding the Embargo Act 7 ships sailed from America and not one escaped capture by either country.

To alleviate the effects on the poor sailor who had suffered from the Embargo Act William Gray, Captain Joseph White, and George Crowninshield gave 2 barrels of flour a week, 100 bushels of corn, biscuits, and rice. They also opened a soup kitchen. The Federalist attorney to the Republican Crowninshield, Supreme Court Judge Joseph Story declared that Gray had true courage and was a great patriot. When the Federalist forced him out of Salem his personal fortune was worth 3 million dollars and he owned 36 ships.

The Central Building in 1805 housed the Custom House. Col. William R. Lee was the collector at the time. The Custom House remained here from 1805-1807. In 1807 William Gray Jr. supported Jefferson's Embargo Act and probably closed the tunnels leading into the building. This act made him highly unfavorable in Salem and he retires to Boston in 1809. The Custom House returns to this building in 1813-1819. In 1819 the Custom House is moved to its current location on Derby street.

In 1818 the Salem Bank, later renamed Salem Savings Bank, was opened with Edward Holyoke as their first president. Joseph White, Joseph Peabody, Benjamin Pickman Jr. , Judge Joseph Story, Jacob Ashton, Moses Townsend acted as the bank's vice presidents. Trustees included Jonathan Hodges, Stephen White, and William Fettyplace. The bank shared the building with the Custom House for a year. At that time the bank was in the Central Building where the Salem Partnership, Haunted Footsteps, and the Trolley Depot are now. Joseph Peabody held the position of president from 1830-1844. In his first year their vault was robbed. In 1844 Nathaniel Silsbee became the president and moved the bank to Pickman Place on the location of the current Downing Building. In 1885 J.J. Perkins ran an antique gallery out of the building. I wonder what he smuggled up through the tunnels to sell to the right customers?

I have not been inside this basement but there is a tunnel leading to this building from the Naumkeag Building plus another leading from the Pickman Derby House. Plus in Salem it was common practice to have a tunnel attached to every Custom House in town...

12. Essex Bank Building
11 Central Street

Built in 1811 by Charles Bulfinch for the Essex Bank. It
is rumored that the National Capital Building that he built
was connected to a tunnel so that members of Congress can
escape through. The Essex Bank was founded in 1792 and
was the first in Essex County. William Gray was its first
president. In 1795 the Essex Bank was in the Samuel Ward
Building where the Gathering Church is today on the corner
of Essex Street and Derby Square. In 1805 they occupied the
Central Building. In 1811 they moved here. In 1817 James
King and Shepard Gray , Cashiers, robbed the bank. The
Essex Bank folded in 1819. In 1831 two former employees
James King and his son James Charles King dies. Their
occupations were Cashier and Book Keeper. They both were
members of the Essex Lodge. The First National Bank, the
office for the American Association for the Advancement
of Science, Custom House, and the Mercantile Bank were
also housed in this building. In 1899 the Salem Fraternity
occupies the building and renovates it to their needs.

Tunnels lead from the Naumkeag Block to this building and continue on to where the old distillery and wharf, built by John Derby, was on Front Street. Also the tunnels lead from the Pickman-Derby Building here. Plus William Gray Jr. had his building on Central Street connected and hired Charles Bulfinch who built the tunnels attached to the nation's Capital Building.

Charles Bulfinch who designed the building and the National Capital.

Tunnel leaving U.S. Capital Building built by Bulfinch.

13. Pickman-Derby Block
213-215 Essex Street; 1 and 7 Derby Square

In 1815 Benjamin Pickman Jr. and his brother-in-law John Derby III purchased Elias Hasket Derby's mansion and the surrounding land from Elias Hasket Derby Jr. before he retired to Londonberry, New Hampshire. They would also develop several properties on the old Derby estate. They had hired Joshua Upham to erect these buildings. He was the mason who built the homes for Joseph "Jr." White and Stephen White.

John Derby III was also one of the merchant's along with Judge Story, Nathaniel Silsbee, Robert Stone, Stephen White, and Joseph Peabody who selected the old Crowninshield property to be the home of the new Customs House in 1819. Benjamin Pickman Jr. was a U.S. Senator from 1803-1811. He married Antis Derby whose mother was Elizabeth Crowninshield.

In 1817 the Pickman-Derby Block was built. In 1874 the tavern Salem House was within its walls. In more recent times Chuck's Steak House operated in this location. When it was Chuck's Steak House they converted a section of the tunnel into a wine cellar. If you walked 8 feet from the corner to the left on the back wall you can see a granite lined tunnel with a arched roof. This tunnel goes in about 8 feet before it is closed off. If you walk from that same corner towards the front of the building on the wall about 15 ft. you will find a door. This door takes you outside. It empties into another section of the tunnel with the same granite walls, but here the roof is removed and a staircase is added to exit the basement to ground level. The same sort of basement entrances can be seen on the corner of Essex and Beckford Streets and the first house on Hamilton Street on the left if you are heading towards Chestnut Street. This tunnel lead to Old Town Hall. The first one takes you towards the Essex Bank Building and the Central Building.

Here are three tunnel entrances throughout town that have been converted into basement entrances. The top is the right side of the Derby-Pickman Building. To the Right is a home across from Hamilton Street on Essex Street. Below is Samuel Cook House at 103 Federal Street. Samuel Cook was the Master of the Salem Marine Society 4 times. Normally you just provide a straight shot out of the basement with a simple staircase. These buildings removed the top of the tunnel and placed the stairs at a ninety degree angle to the basement door.

14. Old Town Hall
32 Derby Square

This was the site of Col. William Browne who was a
loyalist during the Revolutionary War who fled to Canada.
In consequence the state of Massachusetts confiscated
his property and sold it to Elias Hasket Derby in 1784.
This mansion was designed by Charles Bulfinch and later
modified by Samuel McIntire. Charles Bulfinch built the
Capital Building in Washington D.C. , the Essex Bank
Building in Salem, and the tunnels entrances that connect
them. In between the years 1795 and 1799 the mansion was
under construction. Soon after the construction was over
Elias Hasket Derby dies.

   After returning from sea, Elias Hasket Derby Jr. inherits
the mansion and retires into it for 10 years. Did Elias

Hasket Derby Jr. build the tunnels leading from the mansion or were they already there? If they preexisted his return to Salem, did these tunnels inspire him to connect other buildings in town? Either way he will spend the next 10 years filling in the Commons and building an extensive network of tunnels to the old colonial system.

At the end of his ten years with his finances faltering, Elias Hasket Derby Jr. returns to the sea and comes back with a 1,000 Merino sheep. Soon afterwards he moves to Londonberry, N.H. and sells the estate to John Derby III and Benjamin Pickman. The house had been left abandoned for years because of the high cost of sustaining it. Elias Hasket Derby Jr. has the mansion demolished before he sells it.

In 1816 John Derby III and Benjamin Pickman Jr. offer the foundation of the house to the town to have a market place and town hall on the property forever. The town accepts and they have Joshua Upham build Old Town Hall from plans drawn by Charles Bulfinch. Also brick stalls were added to the walkway leading to New Derby Street. These would be demolished at some point and rebuilt in the 1970's which today houses Artist Row. The opening of Old Town Hall was graced with the appearance of James Monroe as he visited Salem. This will be one of many buildings Madison would visit that was connected by the tunnels in town. Old Town Hall served as the city seat till 1836 when the new city hall was built.

Now when you sit in the mens room as the train goes through the tunnel on Washington Street, 2 buildings away, you can feel the wind come through a vent in the back of the stall along with the sound of the wheels running on the track. The back wall of the mens room is in the middle of the building. Access to the front of the basement towards Essex Street is prohibitive. As well as the back corner of the basement facing Lawrence Place. There are several manholes surrounding the property reading "S', "Sewer", and "Drain". Staff on the city electrical building say it is connected to the current Bank Plaza Building and Daniel Low's old Warehouse which houses the Goddess Treasure Chest now.

In 1816 John Derby and Benjamin Pickman Jr. also build the Pickman Building at 22-26 Front Street and 15 Derby Square. 15 Derby Square houses Maria' Sweet Something and the former location of Fiddelhead. The building in which Front Street Coffeehouse is and the needlework shop is in was a later addition. The next row of buildings attached to these two were original along with a third building which stood where the air conditioning unit stands behind the fence.

Pickman_Henfield Building

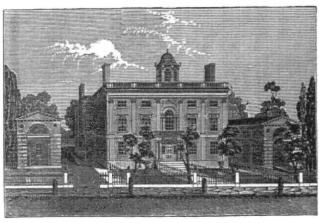

Original sketch of the Derby Mansion that resided on the present location of Old Town Hall. Below is a little door in a locked off section of Old Town Hall that leads to the tunnel entrance leading to Essex street. The entrance was in the floor which has since been poured over by cement.

Market Place Square in its heyday. Most of these buildings are connected to the tunnels. Below is another shot of Old Town Hall.

15. Goddess Treasure Chest
8 Derby Square

From the steps down to the Goddess Treasure Chest to the back of her store and beyond was once part of the tunnel system in town. The sunken atrium shows similar structure as the basement entrance on the Derby-Pickman Building, 104 Bridge Street, and the homes opposite each other on Beckford and Hamilton Streets. As you enter the store and head to the second room you will come to a fire door on the back right corner. Beyond this door is a tunnel that leads to the stairs that exit at a door on Higginson Square. If you go past the stairs you will enter a tunnel that leads to the old Daniel Low Building (Rockefellas Restaurant). This building was once used as a warehouse for Daniel Low. The tunnel allowed him to move stock back and forth from the warehouse to the storefront.

This is in the tunnel leading from Goddess Treasure Chest to Rockefellas (Daniel Low Building).

16. Samuel Ward Lot
Essex Street and Derby Square

The lot was originally developed by Samuel Ward who
had his warehouse on the corner of Essex Street and Derby
Square. He sold the lot that included the next building to
the right, to George Dodge and John Derby (Southern Essex
County Registry Bk 143 Pg 260) in 1785. In 1795 they sell
the left portion of the lot to the Essex Bank (Southern Essex
County Registry Bk 168 pg 70). In 1805 the Essex Bank
will be in the Central Building and in 1811 have their own
building built on Central Street. The Essex Bank will sell
their portion in 1839 to William Kimball. In 1858 Kimball
sells this portion to the Salem Savings Bank. In 1899 the
Kimball Block as it is called then burns down. This will be
the second fire on this location. The first was Young's hat
Shop where th ewidows Beckford and Manning die in. In
1900 W.E Hoyt Company buys the lot and builds the current
building for their clothing and furnishing company. In 1910
Naumkeak Trust Company buys the building. They refit the
interior to better sit their bank.

In 1858 John Derby still owns the right portion of the estate. The building to the right was erected in 1873 and was the first cast-iron faced building in Salem utilizing the technology that would develop into the modern skyscraper. In 1874 the fifth floor was added. The Hale (Mercantile) Building was also bought by the Naumkeag Trust Company in 1910.

This building is a cornucopia of entrances, mazes, trapdoors, and more. Starting in the back left corner is a door that leads into Derby Square facing Old Town Hall. As you walk down these steps and through a little hallway you enter the subbasement of the building. On the right behind what seems to be a furnace is an old tunnel entrance. If you look in the roof here you will see round glass panels set in a piece of wrought iron. This was used to illuminate this entrance while someone looked for their keys to unlock the door into the tunnel. Such light apertures can be seen on entrances to Daniel Low's, the old Sacon Jewelry store basement, and outside the Gulu Gulu. This light aperture is now sealed off by a layer of tar in the flower bed on Derby Square.

If you take a left you will notice how this subbasement was part of the original tunnel. After 4 paces to your right is an arch you can walk through to access an iron staircase bringing you into the basement. Now if you walk till the end of this room and take a right you will enter a small foyer to a bathroom. In the stall to the left is a trapdoor made of heavy marble. If you back track through the foyer to the room and head straight you will enter another level of the basement.

Take a right and head toward Essex Street. In front of you is a bathroom. Its ceiling has a section of bricks displaying the original grade of the sidewalk above. Beyond that is more corrugated steel holding up the sidewalk which is quite rotted. if you leave the bathroom and take a left you enter a room in which the wall facing Essex Street and the wall facing Derby Square is attached to glass panes that stretch 3 feet across the ceiling. They have broke into the tunnel on two sides of this room. When you enter either closet on the wall facing Essex Street you will notice that the rain has pulled the sheetrock off the wall and ceiling exposing the brick of the building and the rubble used to seal the tunnel off.

Now if you leave this room and take a left and quick right you will pass the possible tomb of two runaway slaves. The story goes that somewhere in Salem two gentlemen died and were not allowed a proper burial because their existence might hinder others who longed for freedom. So they encased them in a concrete tomb. There has been an attempt by people in town to consecrate the area as a national memorial, but they failed. In this basement is a 12 foot slab that is 4 feet wide and 3 feet high. It is open in part and then runs under a staircase. It is on the wall where one old basement connected to another. We have had several mediums say this was their final resting place and when someone dug into the base of this slab the basement smelled like dead rats for weeks afterwards.

Take another right again you will find another tunnel entrance within an arch. Under the arch is a hole similar to the one in the Downing Building and the Naumkeag Block. This one is covered by plywood hiding the sewer lines access to the building. In the roof of the arch is a hole similar to all the arched entrance ways to the tunnels. If you exit the arched entrance and head to your right you will enter another room under Mud Puddle Toys. To your left facing Essex Street is a workbench. Above the workbench is a little door that leads you into another tunnel entrance. You have to climb down from the workbench through the door into the tunnel. This shaft goes 12 feet and is littered with building debris. Near the back of the shaft in the ceiling is another hole that terminates into a small manhole in the sidewalk. When you exit the doorway above the workbench you can walk to the back right corner to a stairway to Higginson Square. This is also another sealed tunnel entrance. Between the last two mentioned rooms is a hallway which was the original tunnel that separated the two buildings.

To enter the second half of the basement you must apply to the rear of the building. In the alley way in between the Goddess Treasure Chest and this old building there is an old iron door made to fit a Hobbit. Once inside you climb down an iron ladder. There you will see a subbasement before you with another iron ladder leading you down. Now to your right you will see a window and a sealed off tunnel entrance, made once more for a Hobbit, that is in line with the Goddess Treasure Chest tunnel patio. This would of been the way to enter that building. If you walk to your left you will find two chambers. The one closest to the alley is quite empty and runs to Higginson Alley. The other one goes past another chamber with a spiral stair. Both chambers terminate at a Mosley vault made by the Hamilton company in Ohio where cancelled checks were stored. I give a tour of this building every Thursday at 8 PM. Come on by and see some of the tunnels first hand. Look up Salem Secret underground on Facebook for more info.
Or visit :
www.salemtunneltour.com
to buy tickets.

Here is a view of the roof of the tunnel running along Derby Square. The subbasement off the square has been extended into this section of the tunnel. You can see the glass brick that was used to provide light into the tunnel in the ceiling. Above in the planter it is now paved over.

In the planter you will see the tar and concrete that replaced the roof of the tunnel above the steel and glass plate in the last picture.

Above is the tunnel entrance to the Gathering through the arch. In the picture you will notice the safe deposit boxes from the various banks that occupied these two buildings. to the left is a close up of the tunnel entrance. It extends 12 feet under Essex Street before it is sealed off. A lot of the tunnels have lights running on wooden strips.

Above are two images of the sewage holes that lead into the tunnel. Similar holes can be found in the Downing Block and Naumkeag Block. Below you will see the light above within the arch and the old light port in the sidewalk.

Above to the left is a picture showing the original grade outside the building before they built the current pedestrian brick walkway. Above is corrugated steel holding up the walkway. In the harness you can see some of the original bricks. To the right you can see the trap door leading to the entrance to the tunnel on Derby Square. Below you can see one of the original tunnel arches that led between the various buildings on this lot. Now they are all combined inot a massive basement.

Tunnel running between the two buildings. There is a water main and fire sprinkler system running into the tunnel.

Some people on the Salem Tunnel Tour finding the secret tunnel entrance.

Arches similar to those found in the Downing Block.

People on the Salem Tunnel Tour.

Possible Orb
or just some
dust..

A vault used to
store cancelled
checks. This
is in the
subbasement
accessed from
the secret door
in the alley
way.

In the back alley of the building is a service door that leads to the sealed off tunnel entrance that would of taken you to the tunnel in front of the Goddess Treasure Chest. To the right is that tunnel now used as an entrance to the store.

This is the sealed off tunnel entrance that runs 12 feet behind the secret door above the work bench. It has the same wood strip and light sockets as seen in the tunnel under the chapel in Green Lawn Cemetery.

Lower area in subbasement where the boiler is.

Stairs into the subbasement from the alley. It took me a year to find this missing section of basement. This is one of two secret ways in.

Locals during the Salem Tunnel Tour. One of the only tours people in the city will take!

www.salemtunneltour.com

17. Jacob Rust Store
216-220 Essex Street

This building was built for the Salem Commons Improvement Fund subscriber Jacob Rust in 1801. This is the only remaining storefront remaining from the time of Elias Hasket Derby Jr's tenure at digging tunnels. Jacob rust had owned Rust Wharf that had a prison ship docked there from 1812 to 1815 during the War with England. Jacob Rust house on the corner of Hamilton and Essex Street was also connected to the tunnel along with his neighbor on Beckford Street. Now the building is owned by Cabot Money Management.

The Cabot Farm in north Salem is a private place on a public road. If you are caught walking on that public road with its public park and you wake up the Cabot's guard roosters you are in trouble. Someone from their house will drive up and down the road and they will call the police.

See the Cabots were the second and third millionaires in the country after Derby. That public road is badly humped from the erosion of the tunnel leading from the chapel in Green Lawn Cemetery to their field. Then in their field you can see further erosion as a path raises out of a marsh and then forks to their homes. The path exposes the two tunnels leading to their homes on the farm. The homes have several secret passages in them I am told. Plus they have easy access to the North River where they could land goods to smuggle in town. Or at least their ancestor could of...

This building displays the regular exterior chimneys that can be found on most homes connected by the tunnels. Its the first brick store front from the time of the Salem Commons Improvement Fund subscribers secret tunnel digging expedition.

Green Lawn Chapel which has a tunnel leading to Cabot Farm, one to the west once used to store corpses in the winter, and another leading toward Dearborne Street. This is one of the longest tunnels we still can walk in.

18. Daniel Low Building
231 Essex Street

This was the site of the First Church in Salem and the
Old State House. The State House sat on the corner of
Washington and Essex Streets. The Church sat in from here.
The church was founded in 1629 and has become the first
church regularly organized in the country. The original one
room church was built in 1634. The building was expanded
in 1639 and it was last used in 1670. In 1673 the building
was moved to Boston Street. Now it is behind Plummer Hall
on Essex Street. Francis Peabody found it behind a tannery
on Boston Street and had it moved to its present location.
At one time it was used as an inn. Then in 1670 they built
the second building for worship. In 1718 they built a 3rd
church on this spot. This is also the location where the first
use of a ballot was made in the country.

They were Protestants. Rev. Higginson was the first
Teacher and Rev. Samuel Skelton the first minister. In
1634 the church's third minister was Roger Williams.
He lasted 2 years before he was exiled for believing the
Native Americans should be compensated for the land the
Colonialists stole. So he founded Providence Rhode Island
and created the first Baptist church in America. In 1636
Rev. Hugh Peter took over. In 1641 he left for England
and became Oliver Cromwell's personal Chaplain. What a
mistake, Cromwell was an ass. In 1660 he was charged with
regicide for his involvement in the Execution of Charles
I. He was beheaded after being drawn and quartered. The
next Rev. Was George Downing who returned to England
and became a soldier. Downing Street in London was his
property and now the Prime Minister lives on that road.
Then Rev. John Higginson, Rev. Francis Higginson's son,
presided though the witchcraft trials in 1692. His junior
minister Noyes was ignoble. It was him who really fanned
the flames of the witch hysteria. One of the accused witches
told Noyes "May God give you blood to drink". In 1717
Noyes choked on his own blood and died. The church split
into the North Church and The First Church in 1772. Rev.
Asa Dunbar presided over the First Church. He was Henry
David Thoreau's paternal grandfather. Rev. Barnard who
was the minister of the North Church negotiated with
General Leslie to retreat from Salem in 1775. The church
became the First Congregational Society of Salem in 1824.

In 1826 the current building was built. The first floor was·
used for retail and the second floor for religious ceremonies.
By 1874 a major remodeling was done. The towers were
added and the building extended on Higginson Square. At
that time John P. Peabody sold dry and fancy goods while
Daniel Low had his jewelry store on the Essex Street Side.

The National Exchange Bank had entrances on Washington Street. In 1923 Daniel Low and Company acquired the property in the year the First Church merged with the North Church further down on Essex Street. Daniel Low refitted the tunnel leading to his warehouse on Derby Square. Daniel Low was also an aid to Grand Marshall of the Essex Lodge.

There is one tunnel leading up Washington toward the train station. It is rumored this leads to the Lyceum passing entrances to the city hall and the Kinsman Block. Then leading toward Riley Plaza is a tunnel entrance at the back of a vault leading to the second Asiatic Bank location (Eastern Bank currently). Also Daniel low fixed up the tunnel leading across Higginson Sq. into his warehouse that sits to the right of Old Town Hall (Goddess Treasure Chest). His warehouse has a storefront below street level. The tunnel enters the back of this building and goes up a stair case to a door on Higginson Square. If you pass the staircase it turns right into the submerged store front. The owner of this shop now also owns the condo in the Pickman-Derby Block where the tunnel was turned into a wine cellar. Her basement door exhibits how they can remove the ceiling of the tunnel to expose a cellar door. Few other examples of this can be seen in the McIntire District. Previous to this location here his store was in the Downing Block which is also connected to the tunnels in town.

Daniel Lowe refits his tunnel to his warehouse. He adds brick arches under the flat granite top every 3 feet supported on thick metal straps running across the width of the tunnel. Also he adds thick iron doors. When the Essex Lodge in built in 1918, the previous tunnels under the old Derby Mansion site would be refitted in the same manner.

This is the old sealed off tunnel entrance before the addition was put on.

Some of the glass brick used to allow sunlight to get in to help people work their keys in the tunnel.

This is the door that lead into the tunnel that takes you to Daniel Lows old warehouse (Goddess Treasure Chest). The picture above is just inside this door on the ceiling..

As you pass through the door you will see this nook where one could of laid their lantern down to work their keys.

Here is a picture of me entering the tunnel from the side which used to be Daniel Low's warehouse. The roof is made of a series of arches that run 3ft. and supported by flat iron railings. Below is another angle on the tunnel and another door that might of led to another tunnel, now leads to a peculiar bathroom and staircase. For an old church this basement is filled with surprises still to be found.

This is Higginson Alley. The tunnel bisects this alley to enter the double window and doorway in the center of the picture. The next building in the picture with the fire escape is the Samuel Ward Lot that houses Mud Puddle Toys and the Gathering now. Below is an old vault with a back door heading toward the Asiatic Building (Eastern Bank.).

VIEW ON ESSEX STREET.

19. Stearns Building
101 Washington Street

On this spot was several buildings. Hugh Peters first owned this parcel. He was the Rev. beheaded for regicide in England. Mr. John Orne was able to buy his estate after Rev. Hugh peters left for the mother country with the condition if Peters can reattach his head and sail back to the colonies he has right to buy the estate back. Orne was a carpenter that Peters owed money to for construction of a home. Across from him in 1666 was the first watch house built in Washington Street.

On this spot in 1727 was The Great Tavern which was built on Hugh Peters old estate. It was commonly called the great tavern with many peaks. The Social Library founded by Edward Augustus Holyoke met here first in 1760. The Great Tavern was also named widow Pratt's Tavern of many gables. John Pratt had ran it and his daughter Mrs. Ruth Jeffrey sells it to William Stearns, Major Jonathan Waldo, and Col. Benjamin Pickman. Waldo and Pickman were

Salem Commons Improvement Fund subscribers.

In 1792 Samuel McIntire built the Stearns Building to house the Washington Hall on the upper story and Stearns and Waldo Apothecary on the lower. William Stearns, Major Jonathan Waldo, and Colonel Benjamin Pickman paid for the construction. Major Waldo had repaired Fort Pickering and rededicated in 1799. Pickman and Waldo were Salem Commons Improvement Fund subscribers. William Stearns also help create the Salem Turnpike (Highland Street). Stearns and Pickman die in 1819 as the Great Panic began. The Washington Hall was an assembly hall for Democrats which became a popular social center. The hall was dedicated on his birthday right before his assumption to his second term amid great rejoicing over the success of the French Revolution. Democrats and Jacobins were names of those who supported the French Revolution. Later Washington Hall was used as a theater. Next to it heading northeast on Essex Street was the "Old State House". The Corner Book Store was established here in 1827 ran by William and Stephen B. Ives. In 1851 Henry P. Ives and A.A. Smith ran it till 1861. Then in 1861 Henry runs it himself. They were publishers and book sellers. They had founded the Salem Observer in 1823. The Salem Observer had printed Democratic tendencies within their paper. This building was also the first home of the Salem East India Marine Society.

The Stearns building was partially torn down to accommodate the current Neal and Newhall (Shribman) Building. It was built on the southern portion of the Stearns Building before it was completely torn down in 1902. Up to recently the Fountainside Dinner was here. The tunnel entrance can be seen in the basement in the mens room stall along with the sewer pipe coming up through the floor. This entrance faces Essex street.

20. Asiatic Bank Building
125 Washington Street

On this site was the home of Rev. Higginson who was the
first teacher (1629-1630) of the First Church next door.
Then in 1855 The Asiatic Bank moved out of the Salem East
India Marine Hall and into their new building . The Asiatic
Bank became a National Bank in 1865. The Salem Savings
Bank ,the post office, and the Merchants Bank moved in the
same year. By 1878 the Naumkeag Bank (it had become a
national bank in 1864) had already moved out of the Bowker
Block and into the Asiatic Bank. Plus the Salem Savings
Bank founded by Dr. Edward Holyoke owned the building.
In 1880 the post office was still in this building. The
Naumkeag and Essex Lodge of Oddfellows had their hall
here. In 1910 the top floor was removed and the rest of the
building remodeled. Banks ran by Benjamin Crowninshield,

Dr. Edward Holyoke, William B. Parker, and Stephen White have been in this building. The Naumkeag, Asiatic, and Merchant's Bank have all once been in the Salem East India Marine Hall. All of which have been in buildings connected by tunnels at least twice. The Naumkeag Bank and the Asiatic Bank have been in 3 buildings each that were attached to tunnels.

The Asiatic Bank was founded in 1824 by Joseph S. Cabot. They had Stephen White as a president when they had him build a home for the bank in the new East India Marine Hall.

My assumption that this building was once attached to the tunnels are the facts that there is a tunnel in Higginson Square behind it, all of the banks that resided here had tenures in buildings that were attached by tunnels before moving here, plus the arches in the basement were dry walled over 3 months after the books first printing.

Here is a series of Oddfellows who could of used the tunnels to deliver charity without being seen. (Illustration from A Walk Under Salem)

21. Lawrence Place
133-137 Washington and 34 Front Street

On this spot was the Marston Building which housed a West India Goods Store owned by Samuel R. Hodges.

Lawrence Place was built in 1809 for Capt. Abel Lawrence for his home and distillery. Capt. Lawrence was one of the Masons who reopened the Essex Lodge and a Salem Commons Improvement subscriber. In 1817 the rear ell was added. In 1822 after Lawrence's death the building at 137 Washington and 34 Front Streets (Bleachers complex, Roost, Jonathan's, China Clipper) was torn down. This housed the distillery. The remaining building at 133 Washington Street houses Cafe Graziani. The building at 32 Front Street which is to the rear of this building on Derby Square was added in circa 1870.

This building has found many uses beyond its term as a distillery. It was once a stable owned by David Merritt. Then Merritt & Ashby ran an express carriage and had stables on this lot. On the second floor Daniel Hammond had a Gum Copal cleaning enterprise. In 1841 the Salem Athenaeum was in Lawrence Place. The Essex Historical Society was in this building before it merged with the Essex Institute.

One of the main things smugglers smuggled since the beginning has been molasses and this building was a distillery owned by a Mason and a Salem Commons Improvement Fund subscriber; so it had to be connected by the tunnels in town. Case closed!

One way to find old tunnel entrances is to walk about town when there is a dusting of snow on the ground. The heat from the basement will escape these old entrances and melt the snow on the sidewalk as you can see on the Front Street side of the Lawrence Building.

22. Joshua Ward House
148 Washington Street

This building was built in 1788 for Joshua Ward. Samuel,
Joseph, and Angier McIntire built the home. This house was
built on the original site of Sheriff George Curwin's home.
Curwin was the sheriff during the witchcraft delusion. His
body was buried here under the house until they thought it
was safe to move the body to the Broad Street Cemetery.
The original Town House was to the right of this house
where the Puritans arraigned men for wearing long hair and
high boots and women for long sleeves and lace. In 1789
Washington slept in the Joshua Ward House and School
Lane was forever changed to Washington Street. In the
19th Century it was named the Washington Hotel and now
houses the Higginson Book Company. According to the
Discovery Channel and many other sources this is the most

haunted house in the country.

Joshua Ward was the son of Hannah Derby and his daughter married a daughter of Dr. Edward Augustus Holyoke. He was a distiller and a Salem Common Improvement Fund subscriber. This home has 3 tunnels leading towards Washington Street to his wharf. His wharf stood where the old Salem News building. There are two tunnels leading from the left of the house towards the Dunkin Donuts. There is 3 tunnels leading to the right up Washington Street.

This entrance leads towards the Dunkin Donuts on Washington Street. Entrances like this one could be seen under Mud Puddle Toys and the Joseph White Jr. House on the Commons.

Tunnel entrances leading toward the train station running parallel to Washington Street. One below now houses the heating system for the building. In this basement George Curwin was buried until the fervor over the mistake of the Witch Craft Trials was over. If they found his body they would of torn it to shreds. Later he was exhumed to the Broad Street Cemetery. Now they say the house is haunted. Many TV shows and books examined this house and list it as one of America's most haunted. Plus George Washington slept here while president.

Another tunnel entrance running parallel to Washington Street. Now used to house the furnace.

These are pictures of the three tunnels entrances that led under Washington Street to where Ward's wharf was (Adriatic Restaurant/ Old Salem News Building). The ocean once flowed down front street to this corner. The top one is to the right. The next two are the tunnels to the left and middle.

Back of the Pickman Building next door. See the door leading to the basement. These were not historical but added on later utilizing the tunnel entrances

Two pictures from various times showing the train running above ground in front of the Joshua Ward House. The train submerged only after the house. The train only submerged after the Joshua Ward House so not to disturb his tunnels.

23. Oniels to Gulu-Gulu
118-120 Washington Street to 247 Essex Street

The Peabody and Stearn Building to the Northey Building on Washington and to the building that houses Gulu-Gulu share one large basement. The Peabody and Stearns Building was built in 1882. The Northey Building was torn down and the park on the corner of Washington and Essex Street stands there now. The Western union and New England Telephone and Telegraph was housed in this building. The New England Telephone and Telegraph owned the power Plant on Peabody Street.

On Essex Street outside of the glass window looking into the cafe is a purple glass bricks. These were used to provide light into the tunnel. In 1766 John Appleton's variety retail store was here when Count Rumford worked in it of England. This section of the tunnel has been sheet rocked and turned into an office. To the right of the office is a section of the tunnel still existing. This basement continues around the park to the new restaurant. A new stairs has hindered further progress which would continue all the way to the basement of Cafe Koschu on the corner of Barton Square.

To the left is a picture of part of the tunnel that was used to expand the basement. To the right is a picture of some motley locals who were hiding just to the right. Below is a picture of purple glass bricks that used to illuminate into the tunnel. No longer can you stare into the tunnels below because a drop ceiling was placed below them and the room is sheet rocked as office space. The office is just to the left of the top left photo.

24. City Hall
93 Washington Street

Built in 1836 on the site of Joshua Orne's building by
Richard Bond. Bond will build the stone Court House on the
corner of Federal and Washington Streets later. It was built
by the 1837 US Treasury Surplus ($40,000,000) that was
distributed to the states. It was extended in 1876 and 1979.
This building being the sixth and last Town House.

The original Town House was to the right of the Joshua
Ward House in 1626. The second was in the middle of
School Lane which is now Washington Street. It was built
in 1677 and was used during the witchcraft hysteria. It
would become the watch house that was used up to the

19th century standing across from the Stearns Building just pass Essex Street to the North. The third Town House stood to the right of Daniel Low's on the corner of Essex and Washington Street built in 1720. In 1774 the First Provisional Congress met here with Jon Hancock as Chairman. The capital was then transferred to this building for it became known as the State House, Town house, and Court House. From 1774 to 1778 the Town House was moved into rooms in the First Church next door. In 1785 they met in the basement of Joshua Ward's store where there was many tunnels leading to and fro. In 1786 another Town House was built on a lot that housed a brick school opposite the Tabernacle Church. This Town House was built by Samuel McIntire and Washington had given a speech from its balcony. Then in 1817 it was moved to Old Town Hall on Market Square now known as Derby Square. The previous building was made fire proof to hold court records and continued on its service as the Old Court House. Old Town Hall would be the first hall where the court house was not attached to it. In 1839 the Old Court House was taken down to build the train tunnel through the lot.

A few years ago the city engineer's office received a phone call from a construction crew digging in the alley to the right of City Hall. They had found a large shed buried under the alleyway. They found the tunnel leading into the building. Plus there is a manhole in the sidewalk lining up with the tunnel entrance under Red Lion Smoke Shop. I have a friend who was doing telephone repair work had left a door in the basement of Red Lion Smoke Shop and entered the train tunnel. Unfortunately for him the telephone wires proved to be on top of the building instead. The train tunnel now blocks the way between these two buildings and the Lawrence Branch track is now sealed up from the Eastern Railroad track that the MBTA still uses. The Lawrence Branch Track is the one to the left if you are facing the current train station.

25. Kinsman Building
81 Washington Street

Built in 1882 by George C. Lord for Jon Kinsman who
was successful in railroading and banking. He owned the
Salem Car Company on Bridge Street where Salem Brake
and Clutch is now. He sold his shop to the Eastern Railroad
who used the yard and shops to fix their rail cars. Later he
became the superintendent of the Eastern Railroad with his
offices in the old train station on Riley Square. The Eastern
Railroad was formed in 1836 creating a track from Salem to
Boston. In 1839 the Eastern Railroad extended a branch to
Ipswich and Newburyport in 1840. Did he have something
with the tunnels leading off from the train Tunnel? Could the
sea trade moving to Boston destroy his plans of attaching
the sea to the train to smuggle goods in front of his building
which is one of the only ones to have access to the covered
section of the tunnel at the time? Yes!

The Salem Encampment and the Fraternity Lodge of Oddfellows was in this building. John Kinsman was an Oddfellow himself. These various organization were set up to protect and care for their members and communities at a time when there was no welfare state, trade unions, and national health system to provide help to members when they need it. They were also known for giving anonymously in middle of the night to those in need. Now with this being the hub of all smuggling in town with 5 tunnel entrances from the wharf, did they have access to many goods to redistribute to the poor?

Here one of a series of Bilco doors which were added to the building later. Could all of them have been tunnel entrances. There is still a mysterious ladder behind a locked fence that leads towards the area of this building. Did smuggling get high tech utilizing the trains? Yes! A little late though...

Recently this entrance was closed off.

Center Bilco Door entrance. This used to be one of the tunnel entrance to the rear of the building

Left rear Bilco entrance that once was used to connect another tunnel to this building.

Another shot of the stairs above.

Large Tunnel entrance toward the center left of the basement.
Imagine what they smuggled through this opening!

Strange hole in front of the Bilco entrance to the right rear.

Closed arch to the left of the Large Tunnel Entrance on the opposite page.

As in many of the buildings in Salem, a tunnel will run between buildings. This is the rear facing Salem Green. It is to the far right rear of the building and stretches in the other direction to Essex Street.

Looking toward Washington Street in the tunnel that runs between the two buildings.

The Corrugated ceiling holding up the sidewalk.

Another Furnace opening like the one in the Downing Block tunnel.

Tunnel entrance to Washington Street (leading toward the Mason Lodge) off the tunnel in between buildings.

Above you can see the granite holding up the sidewalk above on Washington Street.

Just outside the tunnel leaving the access point in which the
Kinsman Block utilized.

26. Eastern Railroad Train Tunnel
Under Washington Street from Mill Street to the
Salem Depot

On this location was the wharf that the Port House sat on.
The South River flowed here and went up what is now Canal
Street. Where the post office is now was where Pickering
had his ship building business. Around 1650 Jon and
Jonathan Pickering's ship yard was blocked from the sea
when Walter Price filled the land where Riley Plaza is now
to build the second mill in Salem to grind corn. From this
point a branch split off to a pond near Summer and Chestnut
Street. This was Sweet's Cove where Ruck set up another
shipyard after the mill was completed. This area became
know as Ruck's Village filled with the shipwrights who
worked for him. In 1838 this mill was torn down to build the
station.

In 1832 Thomas H. Perkins amongst others in Salem first petitioned the State to allow a rail to be completed to Boston from Salem. They were rejected because the proposed route would interfere with shipping by sea through various towns. Then in 1835 George Peabody petitioned once more and was successful. The Eastern Railroad was formed in 1836 providing rail service from Salem to Boston. In 1838 the rail was completed and was taking passengers back and forth the two towns. Rails to Marblehead and Ipswich was added in 1839. In 1940 a rail to Newburyport was built. 1848 had seen the erection of a rail to Lawrence by the Essex Railroad which the Eastern Railroad later buys. Then in 1850 a rail to Lowell and another to South Reading opened. The Boston and Maine Eastern Division will buy the Eastern Railroad. From Salem you were able to visit Newcastle and Portsmouth N.H. As well as Portland Maine.

In 1838 a wooden train depot was built where Riley Plaza now stands. The South River flowed east of it and entered Mill Pond which is now Canal Street. Before it was torn down for the later brick structure the walls were black from all of the soot from the trains. The Port House was originally on this spot in 1636 collecting customs for the crown. The first mill built in New England was built where the engine house was in 1664. The Flint Building, built in 1719, was next to it which had the town hall in it and the Essex County District Court. In 1839 an open tunnel ran in the middle of Washington Street. There was two rails running through it. One led to Lawrence the other to Ipswich. Elias Hasket Derby Jr. in 1845 petitioned the state to make a third rail to go through Peabody to Malden and then on to Boston. The state refused and the petition was renewed the next year.

Here is Derby's argument for the new rail "That long

array of cars laden with stone onions and fish ice slippers
and bricks interspersed with passengers moving in slow
procession on their winding way to Boston. They stop at
Danvers for the onions near the Salem pastures to collect the
boulders at Brown's Pond for the ice at Gravesend for the
fish at the Print Works for the slippers and opposite Breed's
Hotel then a well known drinking place in Lynn to receive
the inanimate and moisten the animated clay. I will leave our
friends at this exciting spot and take passage in the regular
train of the Eastern Railroad which whistles by like a rocket
on the air line to Boston." This new express rocket to Boston
never was passed through legislature and they let sleeping
dogs lie in 1848. The Saugus Branch Railroad was created
instead leaving Lynn to Malden to connect to the Boston and
Maine Railroad leading to Boston.

In 1847 the brick and granite edifice was built to house
the train station. This is the popular image we are all
familiar with within Salem. The site chosen was formerly
the Central Dock of the South river (Old Port House) and
to protect the depot from the encroachments of the water
a massive sea wall was originally built. The original plan
included two wings (both are shown on old wood cuts of the
station) but only one of these on the Washington street side
was actually built. It was used as a locomotive round house.
There were three tracks in the depot at first. The middle one
being generally used by the Lawrence branch. An enormous
wood burner Witch No 13 was a favorite train that would
be stored in the station. There were also offices upstairs
extending across the whole breadth of the train shed. The
President, Superintendent , and the branch treasurer's office
was here. The station was first used on December 1, 1847
and was considered at the time one of the finest in New
England. It was modeled after another structure in Britain.

Western Union and American Union had an office in the station. There was a fine restaurant within that catered to the passengers that lasted at least to 1879.

In 1848 six people died on the rail heading for Marblehead at Castle Hill as a the switch man could not get there in time. The train was rushing to hear Daniel Webster's campaign speech in Lynn. Another collision happened in 1862 in Hamilton where 5 were killed. The worst happened in Revere when 30 was killed during a collision. 57 were wounded from that crash also. 1872 two were killed in Seabrook.

Photo: Larry Boccari
See in this picture there was two tracks, the Lawrence and the Newbury Port Branches. The Lawrence Branch has been sealed off along with the entrances to Red Lion Smoke Shop, Essex Lodge, and the court houses on Federal Street

Below to your left is a picture looking inside the train tunnel in front of the Eastern Bank. The Daniel Low Building can be seen to the right. Above is looking at the second train station which replaced the old wooden one. Next you can see the roof of the train tunnel in circa 1950.

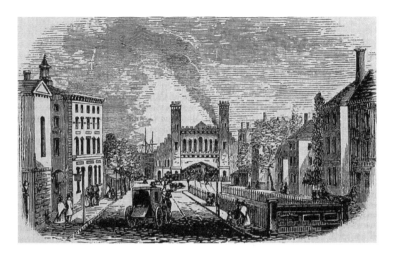

Pictures of the Train Tunnel.

Photos: Larry Boccarri

Model of The Then Proposed Railroad Tunnel Submitted To The Salem
City Government in 1839
The Buildings and streets in the model are marked as follows:

(1) Essex Street (2) Temperance Alley (3) Skulk Alley (4) First Church
(5) Frye Building (6)Engine House (7) Lawrence Building (8) Rust and
Daland Building (9) Henfield Building (10) Rust and Marston Building (11) Ropes Building (12) Neuman Building (13) Nichols Building
(14) Barton Square (15) Marston Building (16)Neal Building (17) Ward
Building (18) Smith Building (19) the Proposed First Tunnel with space
for one, two, or three tracks

Above is an ad for the Eastern Railroad. To the right is the superinten-
dant of the Eastern Railroad, John Kinsman.

27. The Essex Lodge Mason Hall
68-74 Washington Street at Lynde Street

This building was built in 1916 on the site of the Pickman/ Derby/Brookhouse. That mansion was built in 1764 by Col. Benjamin Pickman for his son Clarke Gayton Pickman. By Samuel McIntire. In 1782 Elias Hasket Derby Sr.. moved in to it. He lived here till 1799 when his mansion on Derby Square was completed. His son John Derby owned the mansion after him. In 1835 Robert Brookhouse had bought it from John.

The Lodge had three periods. The Essex Lodge began in 1779 and closed after the Revolutionary War in 1786 because so many had died or were out to sea. The second leg of the Lodge was started in 1791. Joseph Hiller (Master 1791-1793) the customs agent was the Master with Benjamin Hodges (Master 1800-1802), Elias Hasket Derby

Jr., Benjamin Crowninshield, Abel Lawrence (Master 1803), Joseph Vincent, and John Page as members. The Second ran to its close between 1838-1842. In 1831 anti Freemason feeling was rampant in the country. Then in 1838 opinions between elder members and younger were becoming quite contentious. In 1842 the second period of the Essex Lodge came to an end. In 1845 they received their 3rd charter.

When the Lodge started their first tenure in 1779 they were in the Ward Building which was once owned by Blaney at 154 Washington Street . From 1781 to 1782 they occupied the brick school house opposite the Tabernacle Church. This building was torn down to build the Court House that remained in the middle of the road till it was torn down to build the train tunnel. 1806 they were sharing space with the custom house in the Central Building. The Masonic Hall was in the Franklin Building in 1824 when Francis Peabody was master. In 1827 the Masonic Hall was in the Chase Building on Washington Street.

Derby
Mansion

The basement used to house a bomb shelter. Similar to the one in the Asiatic Bank Building. The first tunnel you see is the one behind a metal door. The sliding ceiling bolt was jammed. I spent 10 minutes on opening it. Then the building manager said I could just walk around the wall to the other side... Then if you turn right you can see the tunnel exiting the side of the building onto Lynde Street. What was behind the door was the tunnel exiting the back of the building that was under the covered corridor between the Mason building and the building housing the Griffin Theater. To the right of the metal door is a deep brick lined circular drainage hole. In front of the door is a large covered hole that might of housed an old burner or access to a sub basement. I doubt it could of been a burner for under the Griffin Theater are two enormous boilers. The tunnel behind the metal door has the same supports as can be seen in the Daniel Lowe tunnel with its arches and metal straps. The section under the griffin theater has a sub floor holding the two boilers. In front of them is an incinerator. Its chimney can be seen in the YMCA parking lot.

Metal door leaving the back of the Essex lodge into the tunnel.

Strange hole in front of metal door. Could it once gave access to a sub basement?

Sealed tunnel entrance leading to Lynde Street across from the old bus terminal. You can see the old brick archway at the top.

Lynde Street tunnel entrance.

One of the two boilers.

28. Red Lion Smoke Shop
94 Washington Street

Peck's Building sat on the corner where the store Army
Barracks is now. On the second floor housed the Salem
Cadets Armory for a time. On the first floor was B.F.
Browne apothecary. After this lot was the Pickman-
Derby-Brookhouse estate. The Masonic Lodge sits on
this location now. Where Ben and Jerry's Ice Cream is
was the home of Elder Samuel Sharpe who was the first
commander of the fort in Salem. His home was one of the
claimants of the House of the Seven Gables.

In the 70's my friend was a telephone repair man who
entered the tunnels from the basement of this building.
He met a few hobos and asked them if they had seen any
telephone lines. They replied they did not. He left the
tunnel and found the lines on top of the building instead.
Now this section of the tunnel was blocked off when they
sealed it off around 1991. The Lawrence Branch of the
railroad is now behind a wall.

29. Court Houses
32-36 Federal Street

The "Old Court House" made out of granite was built in
1841. It stands on the corner of Washington and Federal
Streets. The Superior Court next to it made of brick and
brownstone was built in 1861.

The court house used to occupy the same buildings that
the Town House was in up to 1817. Then it took over the
old Town House across from the Tabernacle Church. Then
in 1849 it moved into its current location. From 1849 to
1864 it settled all of the county disputes. The Probate Court
and Registry of Deeds were housed in this building until
they were moved to the left to the current building under

repairs before the new location of the old Baptist Church. This church was built in 1804 and had to move to another building on the lot when they purchased more land giving them frontage on Federal Street. The second part of the church was built in 1806.

In 1864 the Superior Court was built. Daniel Webster and Judge Joseph Story presided over cases in this building.

There is a tunnel running under the Probate Court to the Old Court House on the corner of Washington Street. In the middle of this tunnel is a room that houses photographs of all the murders in Essex County since the late 19th century. Also at one time there was a special stop in the tunnel for judges and special prisoners to be dropped off at. This portion of the train tunnel is now sealed off. But their still remains a fenced off area in the tunnel with a stair case that leads up to the Salem District Court.

The Flint building housed the Salem District Court originally that was south of the old train Station on Washington Street. Later it would be in the Salem Police building on Central street. Now the district court is on the old Oliver Mansion on the corner of Church and Washington Streets.

Bridget Oliver on the death of her husband married Edward Bishop. This is the home Bridget Bishop was dragged out of down Church Street pass the Olde Gaol to Essex Street. In this way they paraded her back to Washington Street to the Town Hall and court. As she eyed the building a large board with several nails in it flew from its position in the building to the other side. Most likely someone carried the board to this location to stand on it to watch her dragged past and it broke with him upon it. Later Hon. Chase Upham when he was a minister of the First Church lived on the lot. It was the First Church who condemned her. On the back of the Oliver estate in the orchard the Salem lyceum was built in 1830. This building would be torn down and the current building housing the restaurant The Lyceum was built in its place at 43 Church Street.

Just north of the Oliver Mansion was Gov. Endicott's Mansion that was brought over from Gloucester when Roger Conant vacated it. This building was once again moved east and another built on the spot where Somerville erected his Indian King Tavern. Later this would be called the Ship Tavern, one of many taverns named this throughout Salem. Up to 1781 it had seen many taverns here that provided "entertainment for man and beast". North of Federal Street was the new school house after the first was torn down to build the Town House in the middle of Washington Street. Before the school was built this lot sat on the North River when Rev George Burdett lived here in 1635. Burdett succeeded Roger Williams as minister of the First Church when Williams was banned from the state for wanting to pay the Indians for their land. This school house has been used as a furniture warehouse amongst other things. Now where the Federal Street Condos are was the Old Bakery at 25 Washington Street and the Holyoke Building at 27 Washington Street which housed the Masonic Lodge for a period of time. Later this area would be torn down to make a building for A&P grocery Store and a bowling alley.

The North River was called by the Indians as " Nahum Kieke". Puritan divines Cotton Mathers and John White thought Nahum to mean comfort in Hebrew and Kieke

Haven. They believed the Jews visited the Indians in time past. The North River flowed to the entrance of the train tunnel under Bridge Street. There was once an old road that followed the North River which was 8 feet wide that ran from Washington to Boston Street. It was closed when Federal Street was built. The portion from Washington to North Street became Marlboro Street through the last of the old forest in Salem. From Washington to Saint Peter Street was County Street.

Across from the court houses is Lynde Street which had fine gardens and homes. Originally built on a swamp Lynde Street housed Rufus Choatte. In this estate on the east side of Lynde Street Hon. William D. Northend occupied him afterward. Rufus Choatte would succeed Daniel Webster in prominence in the Essex Bar. Lynde Street was named after Benjamin Lynde who was Chief Justice of Massachusetts in 1729.

Benjamin Lynde took the oath of the bar in 1701. He owned Lynde Street at the time. In the Arbor Lot of his property contained the first fort in Salem. This fort was built in 1626 by Roger Conant and the Old Planters. The Arbor Lot is about where Sewall Street is now.

-The End-

Tunnel leading from Registry of Deeds. Door in the tunnel pointing towards 24 Lynde Street with cold sill.

Conclusion

So here is the end of the history of the tunnels that were built from 1801 to the mid point of the 19th century in the northeast section of Salem, Ma. I have presented the case of Elias Hasket Derby Jr. coming back to Salem looking for a life of leisure. Free from his fathers control he retired for ten years and let his father's grand mansion fall to ruin. That is what history book say, but I have presented you another case.

During the debates between Democratic-Republicans and the Federalists Salem was split in two. Those who were in power on both sides, the Crowninshields and the Derbys, split the town down the middle and shared the profits equally. Amidst Jefferson's new customs policies enforced by Scottish lads that the rich merchants could not bribe needed Elias Hasket Derby Jr.'s skill to extend the colonial system of smuggler's tunnels.

In 1801 Elias Hasket Derby Jr. had took command of the Second Corp of Cadets which was housed in the Franklin Building owned by the Salem Marine Society. He put these good young lads to work in filling in the creek to the sea from the commons and the several ponds attached to it. He leveled the hills and graded the Commons so he could fence them in and plant rows of poplars to attract his conspirators to move into homes around the perimeter. He needed a large number of 159 subscribers who donated money to the Salem Commons Improvement Fund to build two brick homes at regular intervals around the Commons. After spurious questions of the amount of bricks his grandfather ordered to build his father's home, Elias Hasket Derby Jr. realized he needed men to build two large brick mansions around town at the same time to hide the amount of bricks being purchased to build the tunnels. Also Derby realized he could sneak the dirt from the tunnels into the Commons to help fill in the creek and ponds. These homes would have exterior chimneys that were wasteful in energy costs but useful to attach the tunnels to these homes. The chimneys and their fireplace arches created a weather tight entrance into the homes and drew air through the tunnels from manholes.

These tunnels went through the fireplace arches supporting the chimneys or up through their floors under the arch depending on the grade. These homes off the commons provided for warehouse space for smuggled cargo, routes for merchants to travel to brothels and banks, and in one instance a passage for a murder. On Essex Street these tunnels follow manhole covers marked "S", "Drain", "Sewer", and "SELCO". They enter through simple doors, now bricked up, into the basements of stores and banks on Essex and Washington Streets.

The tunnels provided a way for cargo and money to travel from the wharfs to the stores and banks without paying duties. Tunnel entrances have been found in the back of vaults on Essex Street. Salem in the 19th century had the most millionaires in the country and they did not come to that money fairly.

This group of legal pirates rose from raiding British ships to become Congressmen, Senators, Secretary of State, Secretary of the Navy, Port Inspectors, and Supreme Court Justices. During a time when Federalist tried putting forth doctrine strangely familiar to the 8 year term of George W. Bush. All in efforts to hold onto the fruits of their commerce as the rest of the country paid for the infrastructure that would carry their goods inland. Men connected to the Peabody, White, Derby, Gray, Pickman, Crowninshield, and Hodges families through employment or marriage. These men were part of the Salem Commons Improvement Fund, Salem Marine Society, Salem East India Marine Society, the Essex Masonic Lodge, Essex Institute, Eastern Railroad, and several banks. All working toward the "Great Tax Swindle of our Founding Fathers".

We have read about the famous murder of Captain White that was connected to these tunnels. How they moved runaway slaves to freedom. Men sneaking through them at night to find "Bungholes" to have a nip or two during Prohibition. We touched on the drug baron Thomas Perkins, which some spurious sources attribute to the roots of the Skull and Bones, in our stories about the tunnels. We will expand on him and the drug empire that grew after his death by his family and associates during and after the Opium War in China.

The next book will go into detail about the tunnels connected to the Southwest of Salem along lower Essex Street, Federal Street, Boston Street, the North Fields, and the McIntire District. In this tomb we will ask if the prominence of brick houses had become a sign of luxury or still utilitarian in construction. Starting from Thomas Perkins house on Ash Street we will go further into the underworld of Salem crime and justice. This edition will end on the history of the old jail on Bridge Street.

Till then this first part of the history of the tunnels in town will be printed in regular editions of a few months apart updating the information I find out about the tunnels as they come to light. To help this to happen I encourage you to send me stories and photos of the houses to the Facebook Page "Salem Secret Underground" or my email docterspond@comcast.net. I am looking forward to all of the stories we can dig up together.

Appendix

1801 A.D.

~Thomas Jefferson becomes the 3rd president of the United
    States Congress.

~Elias Hasket Derby Jr. Returns to Salem on the Mount
    Vernon

~Elias Hasket Derby Jr. takes over the Second Corp of
    Cadets.

~Elias Hasket Derby Jr. raises $2,5000 for the Salem
    Commons Improvement with 159 subscribers made
    up of merchants and sea captains.

~The Thomas March House begins construction and will be
    the furthest house to be connected to the tunnels
    from Elias Hasket Derby's brick house on Derby
    Street.

~Jacob Rust Store (216-220 Essex Street) will be built and
    was at the time the furthest store connected to the
    tunnels in 1801.

~Joseph Story is admitted to the Essex Bar.

~Salem East India Marine Society opens their first museum.

159 Commons Improvement Subscribers

1. Elias Hasket Derby Jr.
2. William Prescott
3. Benjamin Pickman (Derby's Brother in-law.)
4. Clifford Crowninshield (his house is on the Commons and dies in 1809 at 47.)
5. Joseph Peabody
6. Thomas Briggs (his ropewalk was removed to Bridge Street and formed part of Stickney's walk and married Vincent's daughter.)
7. John Gray (son of William Gray.)
8. Samuel Archer
9. William Carlton (owner of Salem Gazette and Salem Register who went to jail in 1803 for insulting Col. Pickering who wrote the Alien Sedition Act.)
10. Stephen Webb (brother Benjamin owned the Sun Tavern which is now the Peabody Essex Museum offices. He was a ship Owner.)
11. Nehemiah Adams
12. Walter Bartlett (Auctioneer and first of the subscribers to be deranged)
13. Samuel Webb (Silversmith and 2nd to be deranged.)
14. Mary Boardman (Benjamin Hodges sister. Her other siblings were Gamaliel and George. Their father was John. Her daughter Elizabeth married Nathaniel ` Bowditch . Another daughter Mary married Benjamin W. Crowninshield.)
15. John Babbidge (partners with Jonathan Hawkes who bought the Hawkes house from Derby.)
16. Nathaniel Bowditch
17. William Manning (Owned a stage coach and was Hawthorne's uncle.)
18. John Dutch (baker.)

19. Thadeus Gwinn (ropemaker.)
20. Benjamin West Jr. (Captain.)
21. Jeremiah Shepard (hatter and grocer.)
22. Penn Townsend (Captain, Mason, and revenue agent.)
23. Mary Oliver
24. Benjamin Oliver (doctor and a scientific man.)
25. Peter Oliver (3rd to be deranged.)
26. John Scobbie (Dry Goods business in the Franklin Building.)
27. Benjamin Hodges (Master of Essex Lodge, and 1st president of the Salem East India Marine Society. His son Benjamin dies one year after graduating Harvard in 1804)
28. Thomas Bancroft (Clerk of Courts, 1808 dies as a supercargo)
29. Benjamin Webb (Captain, owned Sun Tavern)
30. Joseph Hiller (Silversmith, customs collector, first master of the Essex Mason Lodge in 1791)
31. Isaac Osgood (lives in John Hodges home, married 3 Pickman daughters, was Clerk of Courts)
32. James Wright (baker.)
33. Ebenezer Putnam
34. Samuel Cheever (Mason,Tanner, and lived on the site of the Hannah Hodges-Joseph White House)
35. Joseph Vincent (senior warden of the Masons and ropemaker)
36. David Murphy (foreman of Briggs ropewalk.)
37. Jesse Richardson (President of an insurance Company, and dies in 1814 at 37.)
38. Jeduthan Upton (baker, merchant, Mason.)
39. Edward Allen (marries Gamaliel Hodges.)
40. Israel Williams (Captain Salem Cadets and sea captain.)
41. John Osgood (Captain.)
42. Joseph Perkins (lawyer and Captain of Cadets.)
43. Jacob Ashton (President of Salem Marine Insurance Co.)

44. Abel Lawrence (distiller, Mason, 4th captain of Salem Cadets, distillery was on front Street, lived on corner of Essex and Barton Square)

45. Amos Hovey (dry goods in the Franklin Building, merchant on Union Wharf, and held several military positions.)

46. Thomas Webb (Captain and keeper of the prison ship on Rust's Wharf during the 1812 War.)

47. Joshua Ward (Essex Lodge was in his house, distiller, son of Hannah Derby Ward, and merchant)

48. Nathan Pierce (Owned Pierce's [Dodge's] Wharf, lost many buildings in the 1816 fire)

49. Martha Derby (Elias Hasket Derby Jr. sister, married John Prince)

50. John Fairfield (merchant and lived in the Mason House where William Roberts lived, in 1814 went to Londonberry and herded sheep for Elias Hasket Derby Jr.)

51. John Jenks (Mason, dry goods, capt. Lieut. Salem Cadets.)

52. Samuel Gray Jr. (shoemaker.)

53. John Derby Jr. (tailor.)

54. Edward Augustus Holyoke (doctor, first president of the Academy of Arts and Sciences, founder of New England Medical Journal, and first dean of Harvard Medical School. One of his daughters married William Turner and the other Joshua Ward)

55. Thomas Lee (Holyoke's neighbor, his house was sold to Benjamin Crombie in 1803 who opened a tavern there.)

56. Jonathan Neal (privateer Captain)

57. William Gray Jr. (merchant, called Bill Gray, worked in Elias Hasket Derby Sr. counting house, his house was the Essex House, Kings Arms, and The Sun Tavern. This was once an old house owned by Col. Benjamin Browne a loyalist. He later moved to Col. William

Browne's old House and moved the Sun Tavern there
[Peabody Essex Museum offices]. William was also a
loyalist and fled the country)

58. Jonathan Gardner Jr. (owned a tan yard in winter street,
incorporated the Salem Marine Society in 1772, and was
a merchant.)

59. Abijah Northey (store owner.)

60. Joseph Waters (Captain of the Essex,commander of
seafencibles during the 1812 War.)

61. John Gibaut (married Sarah Crownisnshield, Collector
for Gloucester)

62. Susannah Archer

63. Sarah Fisk (Gen. John Fiske's wife.)

64. Israel Dodge (merchant and distiller.)

65. Samuel Putnam (Ma. Supreme Judicial Court Judge)

66. Enoch Swett (Captain and Mason)

67. John Andrew (father had a home on the spot of the
Franklin Building, partner in Archer & Andrew, and was
a commission merchant in Russia.)

68. James Devereux (captain, married Sally Crowninshield,
and was a Mason.)

69. Simon Forrester (merchant, owned Central wharf, and
the store opposite of his home on Derby Street.)

70. Thomas Ashby (captain, grocer, home was in between
Curtis and Orange Streets which was owned by his
wife's father Capt. John White.)

71. Moses Little (doctor.)

72. William Appleton (cabinet maker, lived in home on
Harbor and Lafayette Streets.)

73. William Lascomb (painter).

74. Stephen Phillips (Captain, Philips house on Chestnut.)

75. John Watson (school master, his school house was on
the Union/Merchant/Brown Building, his daughter
Abigail married William B. Parker who sired the Parker

Brothers.)

76. Ebenezear Beckford (representative to the General Court.)
77. Moses Townsend (president of the Union Marine Insurance Co., lived in Brick house on corner of Carlton and Derby Streets)
78. William Luscomb Jr. (painter and son of William Luscomb contributor)
79. William Marston (grocer and Captain of militia.)
80. Willard Peele (merchant and president of Commercial Bank)
80. Samuel Buffum (sailmaker partnered to John Howard.)
81. John Howard (sailmaker, president of the Mechanic Association.)
82. Joshua Dodge (married Elizabeth Crowninshield.)
83. Jonathan Mason (Captain and merchant.)
84. Henry Prince (Captain, merchant, his son captained a Revenue cutter, owned the shop in front of the Derby House on Derby Street and the house itself.)
85. Gamaliel Hodges (Captain, merchant, Benjamin Hodges was his brother.)
86. John and Richard Gardner (merchants, carpenters, mother was Sarah Derby, John built the Pingree/ Gardener house in which Captain Joseph White was murdered in.)
87. William Browne & Sons (tan yard that stood on the corner of Andrew and Washington Square East and Deacon of the East Church)
88. Nathaniel Silsbee Jr. (Captain, supercargo, merchant, Senator,and married Mary Crowninshield.)
89. Joshua Orne (merchant, his house was on the spot of City Hall, and was a Mason.)
90. Michael Webb (grocer.)
91. George Crowninshield & Co. (merchants and captains)

92. Richard Manning (Squire Manning, captain, money lender, Justice of the Peace, home was on the current spot of the Phillips School, family had a shoe shop amongst a variety of shops)

93. Edward Norris Jr. (Captain, notary public.)

94. John Treadwell (minister, school master, Representative to General Court, Senator, Judge of Common Pleas Court.)

95. Josiah Richardson (butcher, shop was on the head of Smith Wharf, and home was opposite March Street on Bridge Street.)

96. Timothy Wellman (Captain and lived near the corner of Hardy and Derby Streets)

97. John Norris (merchant, distiller, and left his fortune to the Andover Theological Institution)

98. Peter Lander (president of Merchant Insurance Co., lived east of the East India Marine Hall, and his daughter was a sculptress.)

99. Benjamin Crowninshield (Captain, Collector of Marblehead, and Mason)

100. Jonathan Waldo & Son (apothecary, worked for Stearns, Major of Militia, and Selectman, built brick building on corner of Washington and Essex Streets with Benjamin Pickman and Stearns and Waldo &Co., repaired Fort Pickering in 1799)

101. James Cheever (Captain, Lieutenant of the Grand Turk during Revolution, Selectmen during the Embargo days, and Officer in the Customs House appointed by Jefferson, and lived on the north side of Essex Street opposite Hardy Street)

102. William Ramsdell (Captain for Joseph Peabody and partners with Nathaniel Knight in Knight & Ramsdell.)

103. Benjamin West (Captain)

104. Elijah Haskell (Captain, lost his arm, Inspector of

Customs, lived on Essex opposite Curtis Street, and
his mother was Hannah Silsbee.)

105. Isaac Very (Captain, son Daniel T. dies in Dartmouth
      prison, and was a Mason)

106. Matthew Vincent (Owned the Narborne House on
      Essex Street, foreman of his father's ropewalk, and had
      a twine factory near Pleasant and Spring Street)

107. David Patten (orphan educated by Samuel Silsbee,
      married his daughter, Mason, and was a Captain who
      died at sea in 1805.)

108. Samuel Endicott (captain for Joseph Peabody,
      merchant, and lived at 2 Winter Street.)

109. Daniel Hathorne (Captain, died at sea in 1805 ,at the
      same year David Patten did, at 37, and was a Mason.)

110. Gideon Tucker (clerk and partner with Joseph Peabody,
      and built home on Essex Street)

111. Joseph Vincent Jr. (ropemaker)

112. I. Nichols (merchant and owned the Ware Farm on
      Salem Turnpike)

113. Nathan Pierce Jr.

114. C. Cleveland (deputy Collector under Major Hiller, and
      owned a Insurance Office and Brokerage Company.)

115. William Lang Jr.(auctioneer.)

116. Isaac Smith (Captain, lived in 91 Bridge Street, George
      Hodgkins moved into his house, died in Jamaica in
      1802 at 33, and was a Mason.)

117. Joseph Knapp (Captain, merchant, and lived on the
      south side of Essex Street in between Curtis and
      Orange Streets)

118. John Endicott (Captain who worked for Joseph
      Peabody.)

119. Jonathan Archer (shopkeeper, Assessor, Tax Collector,
      and deacon of East Church.)

120. John Bray and son Daniel (shoemaker, and his daughter

married Captain Benjamin Webb. His son was an
accountant and Lieutenant of Salem Cadets)

121. Jonathan Smith (Block and pump maker who sucked
the water out of the tunnels during construction.)

122. Mysterious donor of $5

123. Henry Tibbets (Captain and Inspector of Customs.)

124. John Derby (lived in what was the Robert Brookhouse
on Washington Street, Brigadier General Elias Hasket
Derby Jr. brother, and dies checking his mail at the Post
Office at 65)

This sum was not large enough so there was a second
fund drive. Some people will give even a second time.

1. George Crowninshield & Sons Co.

2. Jacob Crowninshield (Representative in Congress, dies at
38 in 1808 in Washington after spitting up blood on the
floor of Congress.)

3. Joseph Ropes (Captain.)

4. Daniel Pierce (Captain and lived in a house on the corner
of Essex and Cambridge.)

5. Simon Forrester

6. Stephen Phillips

7. J. Shepard, Samuel Cheever

8. Thomas Briggs

9. Joseph Vincent

10. Benjamin Hodges

11. John Southwick (school master and Representative to
the Courts)

12. B. L. Oliver

13. Samuel Archer

14. Nathaniel West (Captain, privateer, merchant, married

Elizabeth Derby, and lived out his life in his tenement on Summer Street.)

15. John Fairfield
16. William Gray
17. Jacob P. Rust (owned brick shop on Essex which is now Cabot Money Management.)
18. Jabez Baldwin (Jeweler in the West Block, Baldwin & Jones of Boston, and daughter marries Thomas Briggs who lived in the Brick house on Pleasant Street.)
19. Edward Allen Jr. (merchant.)
20. Samuel McIntire (designed the western and eastern gates)
21. Captain Jonathan Hodges (merchant, distiller, Commander of Salem Cadets, and Salem Treasure.)
23. Samuel Archer the 3rd (merchant, captain, Colonel of the Regiment, and he built the Franklin Building.)
24. Joseph Winn (butcher, merchant, and commander of Salem Cadets)
25. George Dean (was a Quaker but became Colonel of the Militia to become a Quaker again and sold hardware)
26. Thomas Whittredge (Captain and his daughter married Tucker Daland.)
27. Bartholomew Putnam (Surveyor of the Port, lived where the East Church or Witch Museum is now, and married Sarah Hodges. Gamaliel's daughter)
28. Captain Joseph White (murdered in his home in 1830, Captain of the Revenge, first privateer from Salem)
29. Jerthmael Peirce (Pierce & Waite)
30. Aaron Waitt (Pierce & Waitt)
31. John Dabney (printer, bookseller, Post Master in the Bowker Block)
32. Benjamin Webb (owner of the Sun Tavern where the Bowker Block is, the estate was sold in 1805 by William Gray to the Union Marine Insurance Company,

afterward the tavern was kept by William Manning, and
Dabney farmed on the North River on Conant Street.)

33. William Merriam (carpenter and later owned the
Commercial Coffee House in Boston)

34. Samuel Skerry (Captain and kicked in the head by a
horse in 1808 in Pope's Stable on Federal Street at the
age of 36)

35. Benjamin Felt (block and Pump Maker also helped
pump out the water while digging the tunnels)

36. Samuel Derby (2nd Captain of Salem Light Infantry,
Colonel of Regiment, and General of Brigade, Mason,
and married 3 times.)

37. Samuel Ropes (ship Chandler in the firm Page & Ropes
and his daughter married Henry Prince.)

38. Benjamin Pickman Jr.

39. Jacob Crowninshield

40. Nathaniel Silsbee

41. B.L. Oliver

42. A Friend

43. Joseph Vincent

44. Nehemiah Adams

45. Ebenezear Putnam

46. Amos Hovey

47. John Osgood

48. Captain James Devereux

49. Captain Clifford Crowninshield

50. C. Felt

51. Captain Stephen Webb

52. Joseph Peabody

53. Jeremiah Sheppard

54. Joseph Hiller

55. Simon Forrester

56. Isaac Osgood

57. S. Putnam

58. Israel Williams
59. Benjamin Pickman
60. Joshua Ward
61. William Luscomb Jr.
62. George Crowninshield & Sons Co.
63. Jacob Ashton
64. Abel Lawrence
65. William Marston
66. William Prescott

Incorporation of the Salem Marine Society

Be it enacted by the Governor, Council and House of
Representatives, That, Jonathan Gardner, Jun., John Ropes,
Samuel Webb, William Lilly, Amos Mansfield, Michael
Driver, ISrael Obear, Edmund Needham, Robert Hale Ives,
Larkin Dodge, William Bartlett, Joseph Lambert, Benjamin
West, Edmund Giles, William Slewman, Samuel Williams,
Josiah Batchelder, John Batten, John Elkins, George
Crowninshield, Edward Gibaut, Joseph Lee, Edward Allen,
Samuel Grant, Jacob Crowninshield, Josiah Orne, Ebenezer
Ward, Jun., Daniel Hawthorne, John Derby, Cabot Gerrish,
George Southard, David Masury, Nathaniel Knight, John
Archer, John Berry, Habakkuk Bowditch, John Bowditch,
Jonathan Webb, John Fisk, William Morgan, Robert Alcock,
Jona. Mason, Stephen Cleveland, Benjamin Warren, Thomas
Frye, Jonathan Lambert, Jun., Henry Higginson, and George
Cabot, the Members of said Society, be incorporated and
made a body politic, for the purpose aforesaid? By the name
of the Marine Society, at Salem, in New England:—and
that they, their associates, and successors, have perpetual
succession by said name, and have a power of making
by-law for the preservation and advancement of said body,
not repugnant to the laws of the government; with penalty,

either of disfranchisement from said Society, or of a mulct not exceeding twenty shillings, or without penalties, as it shall seem most meet; and have leave likewise to make and appoint their common seal, and be liable to be sued, and enable to sue, and make purchases, and take donations, of real and personal estate, for the purpose aforesaid, provided the rents of the real estate, together with the interest of the personal estate, shall not exceed the sum of five hundred pounds per annum; and to manage and dispose of said estate as shall seem fit: And said Society shall have a Master, Deputy Master, Treasurer and Clerk and other officers they shall think proper.

And be it therefore further enacted, That the said Marine Society, shall on the second Thursday in June next, assemble to appoint their first Master, Deputy-Master, Treasurer and Clerk, and other officers as they shall think proper, and their seal, and make by-laws: and said officers shall continue until the last Thursday in October next, on which day the said Marine Society shall meet annually; afterwards on the said last Thursday of October annually, at Salem aforesaid, to choose a Master, Deputy Master, Treasurer and Clerk, and other officers as they shall think proper; and for the admission of new Members, which shall be done by a major vote of the Members present at such annual meeting; and to make, alter and annul their by-laws; and if by reason of any emergency, the business of said annual assembly cannot be completed on said day, they may adjourn once to a short day to finish it, and no more; and said Society shall meet at Salem, on the last Thursday of every month for all other business; and whenever any of the officers of said Society shall die, or be disabled or remove out of the government, others shall be appointed or elected in their room, at the next monthly meeting; and all instruments which said Society shall lawfully make, shall when in the name of said Society, and pursuant to the votes thereof, and signed and delivered by the Master, and sealed with their common seal, bind said Society, and be valid in law. Passed in 1772.

Bibliography

Robinson, John. Visitor's Guide to Salem. Salem, Ma.: The
Essex Institute 1880, 1892, 1894, 1895, 1897

Hunt,Thomas Franklin and Batchelder, Henry Morrill.
Pocket Guide to Salem, Ma. Salem, Ma.:H.P. Ives "Old
Corner Bookstore" 1885

Osgood, Chas S. and Batchelder, Henry Morrill. Historical
Sketch of Salem 1626-1879. Salem, Ma.:Essex Institute
1879

Felt, Joseph B. Annals of Salem Vol. I. Boston, Ma: W.&
S.B. Ives 1845

Webber, Carl Nevins, Winfield S. Old Naumkeag.
Salem,Ma:A.A. Smith & Company and Boston:-Lee &
Shepard 1877

Lawrence, Waters, and Jenkins. Laws of the Salem Marine
Society. Salem, Ma: Observer Steam Book and Job
Printing Rooms 1873

Whipple, George Mantum. History of the Salem light
Infantry from 1805-1890. Salem, Ma:Essex Institute 1890
Essex Institute. The First Half Century of the Landing of
John Endicott at Salem, Massachusetts. Salem, Ma.:
Essex Institute 1878

Historical Collections of the Essex Institute, Volume IV.
Salem,Ma.: G.M. Whipple & A.A. Smith 1862

Ship registers of the District of Salem and Beverly, Massachusetts, 1789-1900. Salem, Ma.:Essex Institute 1906

Vickers, Daniel and Walsh, Vince. Young Men and the Sea: Yankee Seafarers in the Age of Sail. Hartford, Conn.: Yale University Press 2005

Morse, Edward Sylvester. Brief Sketch of the Peabody Academy of Science, Salem Massachusetts [1799-1899]. Salem, Ma.: Publisher Unknown 1900 (Morse was a professor at Princeton University-their press could of printed the edition)

Perley, Sydney. The Essex Antiquarian: A Quarterly Magazine Devoted to the Biography, Genealogy, History and Antiquities of Essex County, Massachusetts Volume VIII and X. Salem, Ma.: The Essex Antiquarian 1904

Rantoul, Robert Samuel. A Collection of Historical and Biographical Pamphlets. Salem, Ma.: Essex Institute 1881

Gray, Edward. William Gray, of Salem, Merchant: a Biographical Sketch. Boston, Ma. and New York, N.Y.: Houghton Mifflin Company and Cambridge,Ma.:The Riverside Press 1914

Cousins, Frank and Riley, Phil Madison. The Colonial Architecture of Salem. Boston:Little, Brown, and Company 1919

Booth, Robert. Death of an Empire:The Rise and Murderous Fall of Salem, America's Richest City. New York,N.Y.: St. Martins Press 1010

Hunt, Freeman and Dana, William B. Merchant's Magazine and Commercial Review, Volume 36. New York, N.Y.: F. Hunt 1857

Whitney, Caspar. Outing, Volume 52. New York, N.Y.: Outing 1908

Lawrence, Robert Means. The Descendants of Major Lawrence of Groton, Massachusetts: With Some Mention of Allied Families. Cambridge, Ma.:Riverside Press 1904

Moore, Margaret B. The Salem World of Nathaniel
Hawthorne. Columbia, Missouri: University of Missouri
Press 2001

Bentley, William. The Diary of William Bentley D.D.,
Pastor of the East Church, Salem, Massachusetts Volume
I 1784-1792. Salem, Ma.: Essex Institute 1905

Bradley, Howard A. and Winans, James Albert. Daniel
Webster and the Salem Murder. Columbia, Mo: Aircraft
Press 1956

Tolles, Bryant F. Jr. and Tolles, Carolyn K. Architecture in
Salem: An Illustrated Guide. Salem, Ma.:Essex Institute
1983

Morrison, Dane Anthony and Schultz, Nancy Lusignan
Salem; Place, Myth, and Memory. Lebanon,
N.H.:Northeastern University Press 2004

Other Books by Christopher Jon Luke Dowgin

A Walk Through Salem
A Walk Under Salem
A Walk Above Salem
Gang Stories
Tyler Moves to Gibsonton, Florida
The Sun, The Moon, and 2 Fish
Jasper: A Bunny's Tale
The Wizard of Lynn

Other Books by Salem Hoouse Press

Ideas for America~ Matthew J. Fraser
Anatomy of a Love Affair~ mi Keaton
Poems and Songs~ Will Pirone
The Ugly European~ Dr. Robert Senn

Salem House Press
www.salemhousepress.com

 Christopher Jon Luke Dowgin is the author of 9 books now, 8 that he illustrated. He has been living in Salem for 21 years listening and collecting stories. Many of which led him to eventually write this book. An on going project he is still investigating houses and mysterious edifices around town that might lead into the tunnels below. He also gives tours of the tunnels and their histories on the Salem Tunnel Tour. Visit his website at www. salemtunneltour.com

A Walk Through Salem

by Christopher Jon Luke Dowgin
The First Book in the Salem Trilogy

The fairy tale and walking tour that brings you into the magical whimsical side of Salem. Where fish fly, tall ships drop anchor next to parking meters, and Vikings storm Dead Horse Beach! Come on a journey with Mr. Zac in which you are the main character. He will introduce you to witches, werewolves, ghosts, and some of Salem's most historic citizens. See the sea train and watch schooners fly through the sky.

Visit our website (www.awalkthroughsalem.com) and access our interactive Google Map that will lead you through the city as you read the book. Also visit Salem to follow to see the real illustrations and sketches used to create the tale in various shops in the city.

A Walk Under Salem

by Christopher Jon Luke Dowgin
The Second Book in the Salem Trilogy

In the sequel to "A walk Through Salem" you once again follow Mr. Zac on a journey to help him locate the stolen Golden Egg before the Boy Emperor of China declares an international war. You will travel through the smuggling tunnels of Salem built by King Derby for the mysterious Salem East India Marine Society who has been smuggling magical items and art treasures for centuries now. You will encounter 7 dwarf ship captains, Captain Nemo, goblins, flying monkeys, Alice, John Dee, Queen Elizabeth, the White Queen, Dante, and a walrus. Will you find the Golden Egg in time?

You can also follow along with this story on your laptop, iPhone, iPad Touch, or Droid phone through Google Maps. The virtual walking tour will show you the path of the tunnels, images of them, old postcards, old photos of Salem, and old historical car crashes from the 40's and 50's. Just go to www.awalkthroughsalem.com!

A Walk Above Salem

by Christopher Jon Luke Dowgin

The Third Book in the Salem Trilogy

In this tale the third book in the Salem Trilogy you will journey into the skies in a Caddy Balloon alongside millions of other readers who think they are safely tucked away in their homes. In fact they will be riding within their own Caddy Balloons next to yours. Once you open the pages of this book you have entered the magical whimsical side of Salem. We have employed a vast network of gremlins to paint what you think is the real world around you to keep you comfortable if you should ever look up from the pages. In fact you might catch them smiling at you if your quick enough to see them before they hide behind the book's cover once more.

So open the front cover and enter this tale about the war between the Salem Boys Fraternity and the Mack Industrial School for Girls. A battle raged from the rooftops using pea shooters and Nerf guns.

Made in the USA
San Bernardino, CA
04 September 2014